"The powerful message that 'self-care isn't selfish' sets the compassionate tone of this guide for teen girls addressing their anxieties. Hemmen provides friendly yet direct and clear guidance on how to move through the process of managing emotions and thoughts to arrive at a more desirable place. Engaging stories from older teens and young adults offer hope that anxieties can be overcome."

> —**Mary K. Alvord, PhD**, psychologist, and coauthor of
> *Conquer Negative Thinking for Teens* and *Resilience Builder*
> *Program for Children and Adolescents*

"*The Teen Girl's Anxiety Survival Guide* first conveys the powerful message that anxious brains are rewired through practicing daily skills. Using a lighthearted and down-to-earth approach, Hemmen then explains in simple yet profound ways how to reduce anxiety and improve overall wellness. Teen girls will naturally absorb the messages in this book through engaging with the numerous activities designed to promote self-reflection and positive self-talk—how cool is that?"

> —**Sheila Achar Josephs, PhD**, psychologist, and author of
> *Helping Your Anxious Teen*

D0121945

"Lucie Hemmen's latest book is an essential guide to help teen girls face their fears, comfort their fears, and challenge distorted thoughts that lead to false alarms. With a compassionate and caring tone, teens can access wisdom that will impact the rest of their lives. Parents will love the idea of having a resource to replace nagging with knowledge they can offer their daughters."

—**Lara Honos-Webb, PhD**, psychologist, speaker, and author *of Six Super Skills for Executive Functioning* and *The Gift of ADHD*

"Another great book for teen girls by Lucie Hemmen! In *The Teen Girl's Anxiety Survival Guide*, Lucie translates effective information into language teenage girls can hear and make sense of. She engages her readers while simultaneously providing tips that work and appeal along with the science and research behind them—a valuable combination!"

—**Lisa M. Schab, LCSW**, psychotherapist; and author of eighteen self-help books, including *The Anxiety Workbook for Teens* and *Put Your Worries Here*

"*The Teen Girl's Anxiety Survival Guide* is a youth's go-to resource for overcoming anxiety and feeling more secure and confident. Lucie Hemmen does an excellent job explaining how to break down and confront anxious fears through powerful, evidence-based behavioral and self-care strategies. *The Teen Girl's Anxiety Survival Guide* is a must-have book for any girl who wants to survive, thrive, and conquer their anxiety."

—**Raychelle Cassada Lohmann, PhD**, counselor, educator, supervisor, clinical mental health counselor, and author of *The Anger Workbook for Teens*

"Lucie Hemmen's *The Teen Girl's Anxiety Survival Guide* offers user-friendly, easily digestible, practical tools and techniques to assist teenage girls (and their loved ones) to move past anxiety and live their best life. This book is written in clear language that impressively balances conveying critical information while still communicating in engaging, teen-friendly language. This book will help teen girls to feel educated, empowered, and ready to face their challenges head-on. I am excited to have this great book as a resource to recommend to my clients and other therapists at my practice."

—**Debra A. Kissen, PhD, MHSA**, CEO of Light on Anxiety CBT Treatment Center

"Lucie Hemmen has created an essential guide for teen girls with anxiety. The book is packed with clear scientific explanations, practical and accessible strategies, and real-talk examples of how to manage anxiety when it arises. I will frequently recommend this book to the teen girls in my practice!"

—**Jamie Micco, PhD, ABPP**, cofounder and managing partner at The Concord Center in Concord, MA; and author of *The Worry Workbook for Teens*

the *i*nstant help
solutions series

Young people today need mental health resources more than ever. That's why New Harbinger created the **Instant Help Solutions Series** especially for teens. Written by leading psychologists, physicians, and professionals, these evidence-based self-help books offer practical tips and strategies for dealing with a variety of mental health issues and life challenges teens face, such as depression, anxiety, bullying, eating disorders, trauma, and self-esteem problems.

Studies have shown that young people who learn healthy coping skills early on are better able to navigate problems later in life. Engaging and easy-to-use, these books provide teens with the tools they need to thrive—at home, at school, and on into adulthood.

This series is part of the **New Harbinger Instant Help Books** imprint, founded by renowned child psychologist Lawrence Shapiro. For a complete list of books in this series, visit newharbinger.com.

the teen girl's **anxiety** survival guide

10 ways to **conquer anxiety** & **feel your best**

LUCIE HEMMEN, PhD

Instant Help Books
An Imprint of New Harbinger Publications, Inc.

Publisher's Note

This publication is designed to provide accurate and authoritative information in regard to the subject matter covered. It is sold with the understanding that the publisher is not engaged in rendering psychological, financial, legal, or other professional services. If expert assistance or counseling is needed, the services of a competent professional should be sought.

In consideration of evolving American English usage standards, and reflecting a commitment to equity for all genders, "they/them" is used in this book to denote singular persons.

Distributed in Canada by Raincoast Books

Copyright © 2021 by Lucie Hemmen
           Instant Help Books
           An imprint of New Harbinger Publications, Inc.
           5674 Shattuck Avenue
           Oakland, CA 94609
           www.newharbinger.com

Cover design by Amy Shoup; Acquired by Jess O'Brien; Edited by Karen Schader

All Rights Reserved

Library of Congress Cataloging-in-Publication Data

Names: Hemmen, Lucie, author.
Title: The teen girl's anxiety survival guide : ten ways to conquer anxiety and feel your best / [Lucie Hemmen].
Description: Oakland, CA : Instant Help Books, an imprint of New Harbinger Publications, Inc., [2021] | Series: The instant help solutions series | Includes bibliographical references.
Identifiers: LCCN 2020031865 (print) | LCCN 2020031866 (ebook) | ISBN 9781684035847 (trade paperback) | ISBN 9781684035854 (pdf) | ISBN 9781684035861 (epub)
Subjects: LCSH: Anxiety in adolescence--Juvenile literature. | Teenage girls--Psychology--Juvenile literature. | Social skills in adolescence--Juvenile literature. | Interpersonal relations in adolescence--Juvenile literature.
Classification: LCC BF724.3.A57 H36 2021 (print) | LCC BF724.3.A57 (ebook) | DDC 155.5/33--dc23
LC record available at https://lccn.loc.gov/2020031865
LC ebook record available at https://lccn.loc.gov/2020031866

Printed in the United States of America

23   22   21

10   9   8   7   6   5   4   3   2   1   First Printing

Contents

Introduction

No one needs to tell a teen girl how stressful life can be. You're fully in the loop and doing the best you can to get through each day. Girls, more than boys, feel a lot of pressure from all directions, and it takes a toll. Exhaustion, frustration, and anxiety are a few of the struggles teen girls bring up most often.

Can you relate to any of the following?

- You value relationships and feel stressed when conflict or drama hits your friend group.

- You value family, yet feel torn between making parents happy and pushing them away. (You don't want to feel so annoyed, you just do.)

- You value academics, but feel stressed by the work and high expectations.

- You want to be happy, yet often feel overwhelmed by negative thoughts and feelings.

- You want to feel confident and accepted, yet often feel stressed about how pretty/hot/fit you are or by how much you fall short. (It's not that you're self-obsessed. You just want to feel okay about yourself so that you have the confidence to be who you want to be.)

- You know social media mostly makes everything feel worse, yet you want to bite the face off anyone who bugs you about it.

Whether you relate to one or all of these examples, things are about to get better. The good news about stress and anxiety is that there is *so* much good news. They are common and treatable. In the chapters ahead, you will learn ten tips that cover the need-to-know, along with advice from girls who've been there and strategies that work.

Because you're busy and don't need more boring reading to do, key information is presented in a fast and fun format that gives you the power you need without adding needless weight to your reading list.

Here's how:

Knowledge is power, so this guide will give you all the need-to-know on anxiety. Some of what you'll learn is so simple you will be shocked. For example, learning that feelings of fear don't mean you're in danger—and how reshuffling all your current habits can help you truly make use of that reality. With help of the tips ahead, you will unlearn all your anxious ways of responding to anxiety and be blown away by how much changes for you when you switch out many of your bad habits for good ones.

Additionally, since many teen girls have a natural interest in psychology, the *Nerd Alert* sections throughout this guide help you grow and nurture your inner psychology nerd. Not only will you understand yourself better, you'll understand the people around you better.

Self-care is power, so this guide will focus you on many, many ways to make self-care the new organizing principle of your life. Here's the way self-care works:

The better your self-care, → the better you feel, → the more confident you feel, → the more assertive you feel, → the more powerful you become, not only with anxiety but *in every aspect of your life!*

Practicing self-care has a million positive side effects. And once you get your routines down, taking care of you will feel like a natural part of who you are and how you show love for yourself.

Strategies are power, because when the anxiety bully pushes you, you're going to start pushing right back. No more quaking and shaking, no more rushing home to your bed and your shows. You go from victim to boss because anxiety doesn't have a chance to gain power when you hit it right between the eyes with one of the many anxiety-slaying strategies offered throughout this guide.

Noodle This sections support you in self-reflection, and *Pen Power* sections invite you to do some writing to help you integrate what you're learning and thinking about. Writing is a little thing that is actually extremely powerful. (There are studies!) To help you get the most out of what you're learning, start an anxiety notebook. It doesn't have to be a beautiful journal—unless that makes things more fun and special for you. It can be a simple notebook, but hopefully one you can designate as special because it will be a go-to aspect of your growth and self-care. Have it close by as you move through each chapter.

Time to get started because you deserve to feel better and it's going to be easier and more fun than you think. Welcome to *The Teen Girl's Anxiety Survival Guide!*

Know Who You're Hanging With

Smile, breathe, and go slowly.

—Thich Nhat Hanh

If you're holding this book because you're struggling with anxiety, you're not alone. Even though the experience feels isolating, anxiety is common and on the rise. While 100 percent of teens experience anxiety, approximately 25 percent have it bad enough to require help. That means any time you count to four in a group of teenagers, statistically one of them feels your pain.

> Lexi, age 15: Anxiety makes me feel like my head is a beehive ... weirdly buzzy. All my thoughts go batsh#% on me and I get trapped in negative thinking spirals that I can't get myself out of.

> Alicia, age 17: I can feel good and confident and then one thing sets me off and I'll start to worry and stress and get stuck on something. My heart starts thumping, my stomach gets a sinking sick feeling, and I feel like I have to leave wherever I am. No matter what I'm doing, it makes me want to go home and crawl into my bed and I do that a lot.

Tessa, age 16: I call anxiety my stalker from hell. Lately I'm not just worried and stressed about all my regular things, like how I'm doing in school and how I'm going to get everything done that I need to do, I get anxiety about the state of the world and the next pandemic. So yeah, not fun. The stalker is never very far away.

These descriptions capture a few of the mean and nasty ways anxiety messes with your mind, your body, your confidence, and your plans. It likes to make you question your relationships, your abilities, your worth, your appearance, your sanity—anything it can get its grubby hands on.

As its special sauce, anxiety enjoys distorting reality by affecting your ability to think well and see things clearly. During a flare-up, it can become very hard to accurately read people, situations, and the true risk of danger involved in whatever is triggering the flare-up. This confusion is caused by anxiety's annoying ability to distress you mentally, physically, emotionally, and behaviorally.

As an example, let's say you're texting with a crush who suddenly drops off in the conversation. You text a question mark and wait … but nothing. You then wonder if you've said something offensive so you reread the text string searching for clues. You think you identify the problem, a comment you made that could have come off wrong. Now your thoughts (mental distress) stimulate a flood of worry (more mental distress), which causes your stomach to sink and your chest to tighten (physical distress). You feel irritable, nervous, scared, embarrassed (emotional distress), and you snap hard on your little sister when she comes into your room to ask an innocent question (behavioral distress).

This is the head-to-toe work of anxiety in action.

Since everyone has different triggers for anxiety, the texting example you just read may not have bothered you at all. Maybe you feel anxiety in different situations—social situations, performance situations, new situations, on the way to the dentist/airport/school—or just out of the blue. Lots of teens describe anxiety as "there when I wake up and with me all day long" as if their RPMs are set too high. Not only uncomfortable, but also exhausting.

BUTTERFLIES AND BULLIES

Anxiety has different ways of affecting people, so five different teens very often have five different ways of describing their symptoms. You may experience anxiety mostly in your body with symptoms such as a tingling sensation, dizziness, stomach upset, nausea, shortness of breath, sweating, cold sweating, a "thumpy" heart, or a full-body weirdness that escapes description.

You may experience it mostly in your mind in the form of negative thoughts, racing thoughts, or that beehive brain-buzz that Lexi describes. Most teens feel a mix and match of both, such as sweating and flushing with negative thoughts and a feeling of dread. Ugh.

Anxiety also comes in different levels of intensity. On a scale of 1 to 10, lower numbers signify lower levels of anxiety. A 3 on the anxiety scale can feel like a case of butterflies in your stomach or chest area. It's not pleasant but it is manageable.

Higher numbers do not conjure images of delicate butterflies. If you're feeling a 7 and climbing, there's not a monarch in sight. High levels of anxiety are really, really exhausting and depressing. They can make your world small because doing things, showing up for things, feels overwhelming. You can even get anxiety about getting anxiety.

One thing's for sure—when anxiety is causing you a case of the big scaries, your thoughts and perceptions get blown off course *along with* the basic yet treasured body functions you've grown to know and love ... like the ability to breathe and feel like your face isn't on fire.

With the power to cause so much discomfort, no wonder you may feel downright bullied by anxiety and its evil ways. No wonder it feels like your personal beehive/stalker/bully from the dark side. It's a total a-hole and not someone you'd ever hang out with willingly.

Wired to Survive

In a nutshell, here's what's happening: Humans are wired to survive, and every feeling you have has survival value. Anger is activating and helps you take care of situations that aren't okay for you. Guilt helps you see where you can improve your behavior. Love and compassion keep you connected, and connection is very favorable to survival. Fear is your response to danger and cues you (rather rudely) to recoil from dangerous situations.

When emotions get your attention, for the right reasons and at the right level of intensity, they're helpful! When they blow up inside you, impacting your thoughts and feelings and behaviors without a valid reason, they cause problems.

Fortunately, your brain, like your phone, has had a few updates over the years. You have a *prefrontal cortex* (PFC), which means you can think, plan, act, create, and live more elaborately than humans did eons ago. The PFC is also the part of your brain that enables you to develop your unique personality.

But not everything in your brain has been updated: you still have your original survival station, which contains your fight-flight-freeze reactions to danger. This primitive part of the brain has one major agenda: survive, survive, survive. It's kind of obsessed that way.

To ensure your survival, you come with a little factory-installed brain alarm in your survival station that, when activated, gets you ready to deal with the threat or danger at hand. Because a little anxiety sharpens focus, this alarm is really useful when it gives you a little nudge—perfect for a math quiz moment.

At higher levels of threat or danger, your body prepares to fight for your life, run for your life, or freeze on the spot until danger passes. Pretty awesome system back in the day when threats included escaping scary things that wanted to eat you.

The Glitch Sitch

These days, not much wants to gobble you up. You know that rationally, thanks to your smarty-pants PFC. You totally get that you're usually safe from death and dismemberment, which makes it extremely annoying and unhelpful to feel the smoke alarm go off full blast when in reality the risk of death is zero. When the anxiety brain glitch occurs and there's no running or fighting to do, it's easy to get stuck in a nasty avalanche of stress hormones that create the experience known as *anxiety*.

Because you're holding this guide, you are probably among the approximately 25 percent of teenagers who have a glitchy or sensitive alarm system. Instead of discerning small threats (like a math quiz) from large threats (your life is in danger), your alarm blasts like a Chihuahua barking at a skateboarder—huge response, little to no actual danger.

If only you could just reset that darn alarm … Oh wait! You can! And you will because that's what this guide is all about. A truly comforting and useful fact about the brain is that it's "plastic," which means it can rewire through practicing new habits.

Let's repeat that because it could not be better news:

Your brain rewires through practicing new habits!

You know what that is? It's hope! It's motivation! And it's tried and true, scientifically rock solid. People rewire all the time, and if you focus on specific ways that you want new wiring, you make that happen. It's not a one-and-done effort, just like you can't go to the gym to work out one day and come home with six-pack abs. You don't practice French for one day and then *parlez vous* up a storm either. Big rewiring involves creating and practicing many new habits. Luckily, you'll grow to know and love your new habits because they feel good, have positive effects, and make you a better, stronger person. They all increase your confidence.

Okay, now you know more about how anxiety works, and you will keep learning more. Let's cover what anxiety is not.

FEAR OF FEAR

Because anxiety provokes fear, it's natural for your mind to go to scary places when you're in a big anxiety flare-up. If you're a creative person, there's no end to the scary ideas your mind has the power to torture you with. Here's what you need to remember: when you're anxious, it's like having a huge magnet glued to your forehead that attracts only anxious and fearful thoughts. Do rational, reasonable, helpful thoughts come your way? Nope, and if someone else tries to bring up more reasonable thoughts, you're likely to reject them.

Anxious thoughts stick and feel true when you're anxious.

Rational thoughts just can't get your attention. As you focus on your negative, anxiety-provoking thoughts, you make interpretations of what's going on. None of these interpretations make you feel better. They make you feel worse, and this circular feeding frenzy of negative thinking and feeling is called *looping*.

You've felt it. It sucks and wears you down. In Tip 3, you'll learn how to break out of anxious thinking cycles. For now, just know that the really depressing and sometimes terrifying conclusions you draw from looping are a product of anxiety—not a reflection of reality!

So just to be clear …

Anxiety is *not*

- proof that you are mentally ill (more on this in a sec),

- evidence of your weakness or weirdness,

- something you're stuck with for life.

The best news is that anxiety isn't even awesome at being a bully. Anxiety on Halloween would look like a grim reaper costume on the outside, hairless dog on the inside, giggling mischievously. It's scary only until you strip it down. The sole reason it has the jump on you now is that you don't know all its tricks and weaknesses.

Just like feeling stuck with any jerk or getting out of any dysfunctional relationship, everything changes when *you* get your power going. This survival guide is dedicated to bringing you into that power.

ZERO TO HERO

Dealing with anxiety feels all bad, and the idea of an upside is hard to imagine. There are a few surprising wins you'll come to appreciate because teens who deal with anxiety are a lot like the heroes in every movie or book you've ever loved.

In your favorite childhood stories, the hero starts out as an underdog who is totally overwhelmed and at the mercy of some difficult situation, threat, challenge, or bully. At the front end of the story's arc, we see our hero suffering and flailing. It's almost painful to witness the big, fat, demoralizing beatdown.

Come on hero, you think to yourself. Enough is enough. She appears to absorb your vibes and agree that something has got to change. This is when the story gets really interesting and fun.

The hero decides to get smarter, so she studies the problem more objectively (knowledge is power). Sometimes she gets help from a teacher or coach or mentor (or this guide!). Then, she initiates a plan to get stronger (self-care is power) and engages fully in a training period that makes her more confident and powerful. Soon, she reenters her situation with enhanced confidence and fierce determination to kick butt.

Of course, it wouldn't be a good story if the challenge wasn't formidable, so the hero has plenty of skills and strategies because, wait for it: strategies are power!

If you're picturing Mulan, Elsa, or Katniss, put them aside for a moment. This is *you*! At the end of this guide, not only will you dominate your challenge with anxiety, all the stuff you learn and all the small changes you make will add up, and you'll feel more badass in every area of your life. A well-deserved perk.

Surprising Anxiety Upsides

At this point, it's an understandable stretch to see anxiety as anything more than a curse, but be open because there are some very surprising upsides. If you know any truly healthy and successful adult living a life you admire, you're going to observe some solid self-care. People can have short-term success without self-care, but in time they pay a price.

Self-Care Skills Are Priceless

In order to live a truly rewarding life, you have to feel good and have healthy lifestyle habits. You don't have to be perfect—but you have to have some solid, healthy routines that are good for your mind and body and soul. Bad self-care, like zoning out to social media for hours or abusing alcohol and drugs to chill out, are not compatible with enduring happiness and success. They are fakey self-care, more like avoidance or distraction, and they threaten true success by creating problems.

Because anxiety is motivating you to consult resources like this guide, you're positioned to become a self-care master and you're not even an adult. That makes you: *ahead of the game.*

So many people struggle with self-care for years or a lifetime, but for you it will feel natural. Not only is self-care healthy and strengthening, it does wonders for your confidence and self-esteem. Teens often say they want to raise their self-esteem and ask the best way to do that. The answer? Yep, self-care. Think about it: Don't you tend to feel good about things you take care of and take care of things you feel good about. (Just think of a relationship or possession you value highly … how do you treat it?)

People often think they will finally get around to treating themselves better when they like themselves more or feel better about themselves.

Actually, it works gangbusters in reverse: Start treating yourself with love and respect and you will begin to feel better and better about yourself. The better you feel about yourself, the more confident you become, the more powerful you are, the better you call off anxiety when you feel its flutter ramping up.

Compassion Is Another Anxiety Perk

The most compassionate people on earth are those who can resonate with the suffering of other people. Because you deal with anxiety, you know what pain is. You know what vulnerability is. You therefore have an increased ability to open your heart to the suffering and vulnerability of other people, in all their forms. You don't have to work at being compassionate. For you, it often comes very easily.

Compassionate people make the world a better place because they have the capacity to care about others in a very deep way. The love and care that comes naturally to you will bless you with rich and meaningful relationships throughout your life. Good relationships are a huge predictor of happiness and life satisfaction, not to mention other goodies like health and even longevity. So again, working with anxiety comes with certain perks.

Right now because you're just beginning your pushback on anxiety, these perks may not trigger a woo-hoo response. Understandable. Just know that your nervous system, which is now functioning on too sensitive a setting, can be strengthened, updated, and reset. People of all ages successfully move out of chronic anxiety all the time. Not only are there success stories, there are *tons and tons* of success stories—and when you learn many of the tips and strategies that will help you leave your old alarm back in the cave, you'll be one of them.

MENTAL HEALTH TRENDING

You are living your teen years at a very interesting point in mental health history. Before as recently as ten years ago, too many people suffering with mental health problems did so in secret, for fear they would be judged, labeled, or rejected. As a result, many people suffered without help and support.

Today, there is much more awareness and much less mental health shaming. Judgment hasn't vanished, and there's a whole lot of room for growth through education and accessible resources—but things are definitely trending in the right direction. Culturally speaking, we're becoming more knowledgeable, accepting, and supportive of mental health problems. Yay for that!

Along with the increase in awareness, there is an increase in an associated phenomenon that's not super helpful. Especially in teens and college-age young people, there's an increase in self-labeling (often inaccurately) with a specific clinical diagnosis or applying the more general label: mentally ill. If this is you or someone you know, a thoughtful pause before labeling is highly recommended.

Especially in these years of big changes in every direction, it's a good idea to suspend labeling and focus your energy on consulting professional resources, practicing self-care, being part of the solution, and talking to trusted adults about what you're experiencing.

Grace, age 17: There is a lot of mental health talk at my school, and I've heard a lot of kids talk about their medications or their mental illness. There was even a time at lunch when two girls argued about whether the other had true depression, and it felt like an awkward competition. I have been in therapy to deal with some anxiety and depression so I think I started to see myself as mentally ill and mentioned it to my therapist.

She said that although I am dealing with some challenges right now, my issues make sense because my life is complex and I am a sensitive person. She said sensitivity is a good thing, especially as I learn more about how to take care of myself and tap into my strengths. She also said I am much more mentally healthy than I am ill and that if I insist on labeling myself, to try something more powerful like "Queen of the Multiverse."

It made me laugh, but I think her point is valid. We agreed that it would be best to give myself time to grow and work on self-care. She also said that a large number of teens outgrow their anxiety, and with the skills I'm learning, she's sure I will be one of them. That optimism and reassurance made me feel a lot better than I was feeling thinking of myself as mentally ill.

A Gentle Touch

If you have a diagnosis or if you've self-diagnosed, you may feel your areas of struggle make sense now that you know more about the specific symptoms characterizing the diagnosis. Just remember that, like Grace, you are still learning and growing and even outgrowing. If you haven't been professionally diagnosed, leave that to a professional. And remember, becoming smarter, stronger, and more strategically powerful is your best focus.

There's strength that comes from facing your vulnerabilities. You are an intricate human, and you are going through a time in life that is known for being stressful and often stormy. No matter what you're struggling with, you're always changing and evolving.

You may feel stuck in certain areas now, but nourish the idea that you have the power to change and grow bigger and stronger than the challenges that hold you back. It's easy to focus on what feels bad and filter out the ways your awesomeness shines, so just keep that in mind and work on being optimistic and gentle with yourself.

Noodle This: Ask yourself how much your sense of identity or self-concept is affected by the anxiety you're dealing with. Do you see it as a challenge or an illness? Try on each just to explore the power of wording and labels.

If you see yourself as ill, weak, or in some way defective or broken, do your very best to ditch that thinking from this point onward. It tends to collapse motivation instead of firing you up.

Acknowledge instead that you are challenged with anxiety or that you are struggling with anxiety. Now, reflect on the aspects of yourself that work! Where are you strong, unique, doing well? Do you give yourself enough credit for all the ways in which you kick ass, or have you been too heavily pathologizing yourself?

Nerd Alert: *Pathologizing* means to view or characterize yourself or anyone as medically or psychologically abnormal.

If you see yourself as pathological, you will feel more helpless—as if you've picked the short straw and now you have to suck it up and deal with the result. If, however, you see yourself as dealing with anxiety, which, while not fun, is also not uncommon and is treatable, how do you feel? The difference is slight, but the second view leaves room for hope and optimism.

Hope + Optimism = Energy!

Energy that you can focus on the work you will be doing to kick anxiety's booty. Okay, you get the point.

SMALL EFFORTS, BIG CHANGES

Even though this book focuses on ten tips, there are actually tips within tips within ideas and suggestions, exercises, and experiments. When it comes to transforming anxiety, all the little things count and add up.

Noodle This: When things feel bad in your life, it's easy to feel bad about yourself. It's easy to feel defined by the pain you're experiencing. From here on, you're going to be careful about noticing when you get stuck in a negative perception of yourself and your life as "all bad." It's not true and it's not helpful.

Right now, think of ten to twenty things that describe you beyond anxiety. Take a few breaths, and tap into a bigger sense of who you are beyond your struggles. Close your eyes for a minute or two as you breathe, and reconnect to who you are beyond your anxiety.

Pen Power: Notebook time! Start writing and don't hold back. Self-love and appreciation are requirements to do the work ahead. Do your best to be lavish.

Hannah, age 13: This is hard because I see only the bad lately, but here are a few:

- I am a good dancer, at least I try hard.

- I like dance and am committed to my dance team.

- I usually have a good attitude (in dance).

- I'm trying to be more outgoing.

- My dog likes me best because I understand her and give her the most attention.

- I feel like I understand why people do the things they do.

- I try to be supportive when my friends are having problems.

- I occasionally go all out with cleaning my room.

- Even though I have anxiety, I like dance performances, which is weird and surprising but good.

This exercise was not easy for Hannah. She shared that it felt awkward to focus on good qualities in herself but admitted it felt better than overfocusing on all her perceived flaws and shortcomings. Hannah agreed to explore notebook assignments because she's committed to giving full effort to feeling better.

Bravery

Interestingly, many teens with anxiety are actually incredibly brave. Hannah has always loved to perform with her dance team, and while she gets butterflies beforehand, they never turn into pterodactyls. She finds this very strange but it's not uncommon. Aliana, who often suffers free-floating anxiety and who has fears of heights, spiders, and bridges is the captain of her high school debate team and has won awards for her efforts.

If you have areas of bravery, allow yourself to really appreciate that bravery without finding ways to downplay how great you are. Also, embrace an attitude of willingness to extend your bravery. Here's why ...

Anxiety Paradox

When you feel very anxious, uncomfortable, awkward, or downright terrified, your natural reaction is to do whatever you need to do to feel relief. Often that means leaving a situation or avoiding it altogether.

Keira, age 19, sometimes feels so anxious on the way to her community college that she turns around and heads for home before making it to her first class. Miranda, age 16, is terrified of air travel and is considering passing on a trip to see her stepsister in Australia this summer. Natalie, age 14, left a school dance after twenty minutes because she felt too anxious and uncomfortable to stay longer. Understandably, it's in human nature to leave or avoid situations that trigger unpleasant emotions, and while that is sometimes okay for the short term, it doesn't work well in the big picture of your life, and here's why.

Anxiety is your brain alarm going off when there is no danger, only discomfort. *Discomfort is not dangerous,* and if you back away from things that make you uncomfortable, you are basically telling your brain alarm that it's doing a great job. You're almost thanking it for being so sensitive.

In reasonable increments, the work ahead will help you select places in your life to fight back against anxiety. You don't have to do everything at once; working on some things is fine.

Pushing Back

Let's take a closer look at Miranda, a teen with the dilemma you just read about. She has chosen to push back on anxiety so that she can go to Australia. Even thinking about it, she feels her alarm go off. Instead of recoiling from the discomfort and canceling her trip, she is starting her pushback by looking at her flight reservation online every day. She's practicing feeling her anxiety while continuing to imagine herself boarding the airplane.

There will be more to Miranda's preparation process, but you get the idea. The paradox of anxiety is that if you obey its bullying techniques, you will become more and more anxious in life. Your bully will have more and more power. Your life will become smaller and smaller, you will become more and more discouraged.

Miranda, age 16: I'm honestly not loving the anxiety I get when looking at my flight info. I also googled images of the exact airplane I'm taking and that too gives me anxiety. But I'm practicing my strategies and now, Day 4 of doing this, I have to say it's getting easier. I have some hope. I'm still scared but if I don't do something to get through this, I know I will feel even worse.

And it will get easier for you too, one tip at a time.

Be a Self-Care Queen

Don't forget to drink some water and get some sun.
You're basically a houseplant with more complicated emotions.

—Author unknown

It's a general truth that what you love, you take care of. When you splurge on a pair of sunglasses, you try to keep track of them. If you have a favorite outfit, you navigate eating a bit more carefully. When it comes to your tech items, you do your best to avoid dropping, scratching, losing, and toilet submerging.

The same goes for living things. If you have a pet you adore, you give your precious angel five-star snuggles. And when it comes to your besties, you put care into being a good friend.

You take care of what you value; you value what you care for.

Now give some thought to the care you give yourself. Honesty time: Do you offer your pet, your friends, your potted minicactus more care than you give yourself?

Syd, age 16: I literally never think about self—care. It's not like I don't shower and cover the basics but I don't go to extra trouble for, like, a bubble bath or whatever. That's what you're

talking about right? I'm not even sure what self–care is.
(Laughing)

Lily, age 14: I'm good with some self–care but I think
I could be better. I like making DIY face masks and deep hair
conditioners—it's fun and it makes me feel good. I make an
occasional smoothie with protein powder. Does that qualify?

Molly, age 15: I'm way better to my friends than I am to
myself. I don't even know where to start with myself.
I try to get sleep because I feel horrible without it but it's
hard because my brain never turns off. When I'm stressed,
I like to bake but I'm not sure that's self–care.

SELF-CARE ISN'T SELFISH

You've probably seen a commercial showing someone at the top of a
mountain, feeling like a boss, enjoying the amazing view, and experiencing the sense of pride that comes from climbing a big, fat mountain. Your
path toward living an anxiety-free life will be achieved in exactly the
same way: *one step at a time.*

Beating anxiety is not a one-and-done quick fix but more of a tons-
of-tiny-tweaks scenario. Keep this in mind because it means that all steps
you take are significant and move you toward your goal—feeling good.
Whether you're climbing a mountain or claiming your best life, making
things happen is a whole bunch of steps that you don't give up on.

Many teen girls put loving energy into so many areas of life, yet forget
to give love and care to themselves. If flopping onto your bed in a

semifetal position with a bag of chips is an example of your self-care, it's time to think more extensively about the way you deserve to be treated.

While self-care is good for everyone, it is crucial for girls who deal with anxiety. We're not talking "a good idea" or "highly recommended." We're talking crucial! You may wonder, *What does self-care have to do with beating anxiety? I want to get rid of this problem, not add more to my life than I'm already doing.*

Here's how it works:

> Picture a really pretty clear and empty glass vase. Now drop pebbles into the vase, one by one. Really beautiful pebbles that eventually lean and stack on one another until the vase is full. Big reveal? You are the vase, and the pebbles are the self-care practices you add to your life, one by one. Each one matters and each one adds to the fullness of your health.

Yes, new practices take a while before they feel really natural and easy, but you've done harder things. You're fighting anxiety, and that's way harder than adding self-care practices to your life! As you fill your vase with pebbles, you create a life that includes self-love and kindness one step, one pebble at a time. And don't forget what you learned in Tip 1:

> *Your brain rewires through practicing new habits.*

By practicing self-care every day, you're resetting your brain alarm. You're giving your nervous system a makeover that allows you to feel your best.

Self-Esteem Boost

Self-esteem is a term that refers to the general way you feel about yourself. Healthy self-esteem means that you overall feel pretty good about yourself and value your good qualities in a positive yet realistic way. If you're like a lot of teen girls, you wish your self-esteem was higher because it would be a relief to feel better about yourself. Self-doubt is agonizing.

You can't always tell from looking at a girl how she feels about herself or how much anxiety she deals with because girls often put enormous energy into hiding their insecurities and vulnerabilities. Sure, some girls let it all out there, but not most. Most teen girls are burning emotional calories trying to appear "normal."

The secret to raising self-esteem is much simpler than you think. The absolute best way to raise your self-esteem is through self-care. And now you know why:

What you care for, you value!

This means if you're not feeling great about yourself now, self-care is even more important because it's the absolute best road to feeling better about yourself.

Since Anxiety hangs out with a posse of other heavyhearted characters such as Sadness, Guilt, and Hopelessness, you'll notice those guys fading too. When painful feelings do arise, you'll be able to let them pass through you like waves in the ocean because the ocean doesn't mistake itself for the waves. Waves are surface level—they come and go and are affected by many factors. You are the ocean, not the waves.

NOT JUST BUBBLE BATHS AND BROWNIE BITES

As you can tell by the teen talk above, there's often confusion when it comes to the topic of self-care. It's trending lately and that's a good thing, but the topic has more depth than many people realize, so let's get it covered right now.

Self-care is anything you do for yourself that increases your health and well-being.

A bubble bath and baking both qualify if, for *you*, they increase health and well-being. If you detest taking baths or you've been on a sugar bender, you're better off choosing different options. Taking time in the shower to relax and enjoy it or experimenting with baking by adding or substituting a nutritious ingredient are examples of steps in the self-care direction.

When it comes to the many ways to rejuvenate your mind and body, one girl's smoothie is another girl's nature walk. Self-care practices are as personal and unique as the girl who chooses them. From DIY facial scrubs to power napping in your favorite blanket, it's time to start identifying self-care that nourishes you.

Self-care practices fall along a broad and colorful spectrum ranging from big-ticket basics to subtle self-care choices. Let's start by tackling the big-ticket self-care items that all girls need.

Picture self-care as a pyramid with the big-ticket items as the base. Before building upward, the base must be strong and solid. Sleep, exercise, nutrition, and mindfulness are the four big-ticket items essential in your self-care program. You probably already know that. Now find out exactly why so that you can choose these things not because an adult is hounding you, but because you're taking full and sacred responsibility for feeling good!

BIG TICKET #1: DEEP IN SLEEP

Research shows that sleeping nine hours and twenty-five minutes is optimal for your growing teen brain. Without burying you in details, the nutshell on sleep is that your mood will be better when you sleep that length of time (or close to it), *and* you will learn better and remember more at school the next day. Your body will also stay healthier, you'll be less likely to be grumpy, less likely to make impulsive food choices, and pretty much everything in your life will have a better chance of going the way you want it to.

Magical things happen while you're asleep that prepare you to be the calmest, sharpest, best version of yourself. Sleep helps your brain and nervous system fire down, retune, and reboot so you can be on point academically, socially, and emotionally.

In contrast, if you start your day exhausted, you can't be your best. Tired teens are moodier, more irritable, and less focused, all of which affect your ability to feel strong in the face of your daily challenges. Worst of all, the more exhausted you are, the more you hand yourself over to anxiety. Anxiety and sleep deprivation go together.

Sleep Tips from College Queens

As mentioned in Tip 1, many, many people successfully beat anxiety, and for every success story, there are lots of ideas that can work for you too.

Angel, age 21: My life got much better when I started taking sleep seriously. I have a routine that helps me fall asleep and I recommend creating a routine to every teen girl. Here's mine:

> One hour before bed: *Make tea, putter around my room, clean up a little, prepare for next day.*

> Half hour before bed: *All tech off, phone in my desk drawer. Wash face, brush teeth.*

> Fifteen minutes before bed: *Get in bed, read feel-good book.*

> Sleep time: *Turn on sound machine, practice good self-talk, drift off. Sometimes I think about what I'm grateful for so my mind doesn't derail into worrying. If I get stuck on a worry or negative thought, I write it down on a pad of paper I keep by my bed. It helps me feel like I did something productive about whatever I'm obsessing about.*

Bailey, age 20: My roommate laughs at me but I'm seriously a sleep queen. I have to be. I'm a bio major, and my classes are hard, so sleep is everything or I can't focus. My biggest recommendation for younger girls is to get off your technology because it will not help you sleep. It's the worst and it's hard but you need to cut yourself off or it's like you're feeding anxiety right before you want to turn your brain off. It just doesn't work. I wear eyeshades and earplugs, and I listen to a meditation app on my phone. The eyeshades help me shut out light and my phone so I can just listen to the meditation and drift off.

Pushing Through

Noodle This: Think of a routine to try tonight. It can be as unique as you are but gear it toward ramping down your nervous system. Make adjustments as needed to create a routine that works for you.

Nerd Alert: There's a physiological reason teens often say they're not ready to go to sleep yet. Something called *phase shift* occurs in the teen years, which means your brain releases *melatonin* (a sleep-inducing brain chemical) a full ninety minutes later than the brains of adults or kids.

Even with scientific explanations, it's not easy to make changes as you work to build more sleep into your self-care—but you can do it! You can do hard things, challenging things, without backing down. And it's worth it to beat anxiety.

In general, whenever you are challenged by something really hard, decide if it will add value to your life. And if it will, suck it up, Buttercup, and do the hard thing, whether it's getting more sleep or something else. There are plenty of people who just quit when challenged, but some people push through. Be a person who pushes through.

Noodle This: Tell yourself, *I can do hard things.* Tell yourself this throughout the day, *every* day, and consider writing it in your journal. Why let negative thoughts get all the attention? Focus on thoughts that help you.

These additional sleep tips can help:

- Turn off anything with lights at least thirty minutes prior to sleeping.

- Keep your room quiet, dark, and comfortable.

- Take a hot shower or bath before bed.

- Explore meditation apps like Headspace and Calm.

- Make sure the temp of your room is cool without being cold.

- Limit or completely remove caffeine from your life.

- Keep a pad of paper by your bed and jot down any thought that's keeping you awake—you can get back to it in the morning.

- If you aren't getting anywhere near nine hours twenty-five minutes of sleep, improve your get-to-bed time fifteen minutes at a time. Small increments of improvement will be easier and more realistic.

- Practice regarding your sleep with more respect. See it as positive and your friend.

BIG TICKET #2: MOVING RIGHT ALONG

Another big-ticket item is exercise, a scientifically proven mood booster and self-esteem booster. Exercise not only decreases symptoms of both depression and anxiety but also fires up *endorphin* levels, your "feel-good" chemicals that produce a sense of well-being. Even moderate exercise throughout the week improves depression and anxiety, so much so that some doctors recommend anxiety sufferers exercise regularly before considering medication.

You don't have to become a gym junkie, but you do need to move your body every day for twenty minutes or more. Whether anxiety is lurking or pouncing, getting your body moving pushes anxiety out of your system by filling your mind and body with the good energy you generate through movement.

Every time you allocate time and energy for exercise, you are yanking power and control away from anxiety and keeping it for yourself. Exercise energy is good energy, especially when you get into your routine by choosing the right activities for you. Here's what college freshman Dahlia, age 19, has to say:

> Exercise is the key to my confidence, my focus in classes, even my ability to sleep. In high school, I had a big problem with anxiety until my senior year when I started exercising consistently. I actually started working out because I wanted to be fit, but the bigger win was that it helped with my anxiety. Now I just accept that exercise is a way of life. I love college but there have been a lot of adjustments and opportunities to stress out. Exercise helps me deal and manage anxiety.

Nerd Alert: *Neurogenesis* is the ability to create new brain cells. Research on mice and humans shows that exercise promotes neurogenesis, meaning it improves your overall brain performance.

Exercise also boosts creativity and mental energy, so when you're in need of a little inspiration, instead of a social media break you're better off with a power walk. Don't feel like seeing other humans? Try a dance party in your room and don't hold back. Breaking a sweat is a win!

Don't Overthink It, Just Start

Start by looking at your day and seeing where you can insert a fast-paced walk for twenty minutes. Walking is the least expensive, most accessible form of exercise. If you're up for it, do a walk-jog, switching from walking to a light run, then back to walking in a manner that pushes you a bit without making you miserable.

Your goal here is to get into a routine of exercising daily, and in order to stick with this goal, you want it to feel tolerable. Consistency is more important than intensity because you will naturally build strength and endurance over time. Your body knows exactly what to do—your part is to get yourself moving.

Exercise Tips from Real Girls

Natalia, age 16: I started walking my dog every day after school, before homework. It helps me transition from my day to home, and it makes my dog happy and my mom happy because I'm taking care of me and the dog at the same time.

Ariana, age 16: I don't like to exercise in front of other people so I do YouTube yoga videos in my room. I record all my exercise in my journal as a way of staying accountable.

Lauren, age 17: I joined a gym with one of my friends and we harass each other into going. Now that I've been doing this awhile and feel so much better, it feels weird when I don't go, so I'll go even if she flakes.

Nerd Alert: According to some studies, regular exercise works as well as medication for some people to reduce symptoms of anxiety and depression, and the effects can be long lasting. One vigorous exercise session can help alleviate symptoms for hours.

BIG TICKET #3: EAT TO BEAT ANXIETY

If you're like a lot of teen girls, you may be more stressed about eating than you were when you were younger. Younger girls don't usually question their appearance the way teen girls do, and so their eating is much more natural, and much less stressful.

As girls hit middle school, appearance feels like it matters so much more, and the pressure girls feel provokes self-doubt and anxiety. To make matters more complicated, teen girls often don't see themselves accurately, overperceiving physical imperfections and filtering out strengths and positive qualities.

Noodle This: Take a quick moment to reflect right now: Do you identify with anything being described here?

If you eat regularly and reasonably nutritionally, that's great, because this part of self-care will be easy for you. If you feel an internal tug-of-war between eating and not eating, or feel guilty after eating (known as Food Guilt), or are just plain confused about what you should be eating, this information will be helpful.

Professional Food Facts

Christina Gaunce, a registered dietitian who works with teen girls, offers these supportive suggestions:

Eat regularly throughout the day. Have three balanced meals a day plus two to three balanced snacks. Eating every two and a half to three and a half hours will help stabilize your energy level, mood, and anxiety. If you are not used to eating this way, it may seem weird at first, but your body will adjust and the benefits are numerous:

increased metabolism, improved digestion, less likely to overeat, decreased risk of type 2 diabetes, and more.

Nourish yourself by balancing meals. Remember the food groups? Carbs, proteins, fruits, vegetables, fats, and dairy. A balanced meal includes carbs, proteins or dairy, fruits or vegetables, and fats. Healthy balanced snacks include two to three of the food groups.

Respect breakfast. If eating in the morning sounds nauseating, try miso soup, which you can make easily with miso paste from your grocery store. Just add hot water. Easy squeezy and it gets something into your system before school.

Take pleasure in eating. There are no "bad" foods, just foods that have lots of or little micro- and/or macronutrients. All foods can fit into a balanced and healthy day of eating. Prioritize nutritious foods, but don't make any food "bad," or you'll just want it more and overindulge when you finally break down. Incorporate the foods you love in a balanced way.

Eat mindfully. Observe the tastes, textures, and smell of what you're eating. When you eat mindfully, you'll feel more satisfied and connected. It can even improve digestion. When you're snacking, make sure to enjoy your snack by sitting down to eat and giving yourself a reasonable portion to enjoy. Avoid zombie eating mode by putting down your devices and giving all your attention to eating.

Don't diet, and avoid counting calories. Restricting food is not self-love, it's deprivation, and the bottom line is that it doesn't work. People who diet are more likely to gain weight over time than lose weight. And diets feed anxiety and often trigger disordered eating problems that can be very hard to shake. Choosing nutritious food that you eat mindfully *is* self-love.

Tune into what your body tells you. When you tune into your body, it will tell you what nutrients or foods it needs and how much. If you're hangry, then you waited a little too long to eat. Try to notice the signs of hunger that come before feeling hangry. If you feel physically satisfied or full but there is more of your favorite food left in front of you, stop. Eating to the point of being uncomfortably full is not a loving action toward your body.

Skip caffeine. Drinking a caffeinated beverage is a surefire way to spike anxiety, give you the jitters, or disrupt your sleep cycle. Stick with water and caffeine-free herbal teas like mint, chamomile, lavender, or ginger.

Be prepared. Planning and packing meals and snacks in the morning or the night before will help you be successful in nourishing your body.

Carry a piece of fruit in your backpack always. Low blood sugar can trigger anxiety, and eating an orange when you feel kind of spacey can save the day.

Ask for support. Let your parent know what your nutrition goals are. Make a grocery list and/or go grocery shopping with your parent. Ask your parent to help you achieve your nutrition goal by cooking balanced family meals.

Noodle This: Anxiety is often experienced as uncomfortable sensations in your body. Its physical effects can make it hard to know if your body is hungry, satisfied, or full. Do feelings of anxiety sometimes trigger you to snack endlessly or, the opposite, avoid eating?

See if you can become more aware of your body's physical sensations. If you feel a pang in your stomach, take the time to pause and get to know that feeling so you can decipher whether it's hunger, nervousness, excitement, the onset of cramps, or something else. Each possibility entails a different way of responding, and if you take a moment to pause and explore, you'll get the best sense of what you need. Nervousness doesn't necessarily want a banana with peanut butter, but hunger does! Becoming friends with your body and all its sensations is part of the emotional intelligence that makes you a true self-care queen.

Special Note: Some girls feel a huge amount of stress and preoccupation with food and body image. If this is you, talk to a parent about consulting a dietitian for expert information and guidelines about what you need to eat for your optimal health.

Many teens girls are shocked to learn they should actually be eating more than they think. When these teens begin eating enough of the right choices, they find their obsession about food settles down and they feel so much better.

BIG TICKET #4: LIVE FULLY IN THE NOW

If you don't already know about *mindfulness meditation practice*, now is the time to embrace it. Lots of research—even brain imaging—shows that mindfulness *increases* your sense of well-being and *decreases* anxiety. In a nutshell, it is the state of mind you experience when you're fully in the present moment; calmly accepting and acknowledging your thoughts, feelings, and sensations; and paying full attention to all the information you register through your five senses. This two-for-one self-care practice calms an anxious flare-up while also nourishing your body.

This orange meditation is an example of a mindfulness meditation practice:

- Put an orange in your backpack and go somewhere quiet. (You can use other foods, but oranges are particularly great—many people feel calmed by the smell of citrus, especially orange.)

- Take out the orange and peel it, giving complete attention to what you see. Truly behold that orange, noticing the tiny pores, its color and shape, everything your eyes can drink in.

- Pay attention to what you feel as you dig your finger into the peel and begin to free the fruit inside.

- Notice the smell of the orange and inhale deeply. Notice any sounds that accompany your activity.

- Notice the taste of each orange section. Eat slowly, making sure to drink in all that your senses are registering.

- Finally, notice how you feel.

Mindfulness meditation is a wonderful practice you can use anytime with any activity. Time to make your bed? Try doing it mindfully, tuning into all five senses, and you've just practiced meditation. Over time, practicing mindfulness will make you feel calmer and more grounded.

THE SELF-CARE CHALLENGE

The self-care challenge is simple. All you have to do is add and subtract.

Every day for thirty days, add one self-care action that is beneficial to you. And every day for thirty days, subtract one action a day that is non-beneficial; that is, it does *not* benefit you.

Notice we are using the terms "beneficial" and "nonbeneficial," not "good" and "bad." That's because there's no need to get judgy with yourself. Just think about choices that boost your best health/well-being and acts that diminish your best health/well-being. Add more beneficial choices, and remove or take a break from nonbeneficial choices.

Pen Power: As you progress with your addition and subtraction, record the information in your anxiety notebook in whatever way you want. Jen, age 13, records all her "adds" with plus signs and a purple pen and all her "subtracts" with minus signs and a red pen.

Aside from the big-ticket items, there are millions of little ways you can take care of yourself. We will call them *subtle self-care* practices. Subtle self-care is an endlessly fun topic because teen girls can be very creative and unique. You might think of the subtle realm of caring for yourself as the lemon in your water, the kale in your smoothie, the mango coconut lotion on your legs. You get the point. It's those little things that make your soul smile that we'll talk more about in Tip 7.

Give Your Mind a Makeover

*Negative thinking habits feed anxiety like horse poop feeds barn flies.
In order to move the flies out of the barn, you need to clean up the poop.*

—Luca Tahooley

Now that you're getting the hang of consistent self-care, it's time to address your negative thinking habits, also called thinking mistakes or *cognitive distortions*. Negative thinking habits are ways that your thoughts convince you of things that aren't actually true. The thoughts then trigger anxiety, which triggers you to pull back from things in life you'd actually be open to (and even enjoy) if it weren't for the thinking mistakes!

Most people have some negative thinking habits, but people with anxiety tend to have *lots*—because anxiety can't exist without them.

Nerd Alert: Brain research suggests that when you engage in thinking mistakes, you activate the smoke alarm—officially named the *amygdala*—that you learned about in Tip 1.

Thinking mistakes flip your smoke alarm to danger mode even when there's no smoke and zero danger. You know what comes next: a-n-x-i-e-t-y! Learning about thinking mistakes and how to change them gives you the power to keep your smoke alarm on off mode.

A IS FOR AWARENESS

Awareness is about noticing and observing. *Self-awareness* is about noticing and observing yourself—*in an open and gentle way*. When you practice observing your thoughts, your emotions, and your interactions, you strengthen self-awareness, which is a total win because you can't modify or change what you're not aware of.

Observer Mode

The trick to working on self-awareness is to pay attention to what's actually happening, what your eyes are observing, as opposed to what your fear-based thoughts are telling you. Fear is not the most trustworthy of emotions. It's a drama queen that blows up the negative and makes you feel weak.

When you pay attention to what's actually happening, you're a reporter, not a drama queen. You note facts, not fears. Instead of *OMG, he opened my snapchat but didn't respond … he thinks I'm annoying*, you pivot to your rational mind that notes, *I snapchatted him and can see that he opened my snapchat. He hasn't responded yet. I have no idea why. I can redirect my focus to something else instead of conjuring up upsetting possibilities.*

Observer mode = paying attention to objective facts.

Start working on your reporter mode right away.

Emme, age 20: I love reporter mode. My roommate was freaking out because her girlfriend went backpacking and didn't call her for three days. She basically contemplated every scenario possible, but I just kept bringing her back to the facts of the situation. Turns out her girlfriend dropped and broke her phone but was fine. I helped my roomie keep her sanity with reporter mode.

You know those moments when you really want to help an upset friend but don't know what to say? An added perk to learning to work with thinking mistakes is that it helps you help friends.

Be the Boss of Your Thoughts

Growing your self-awareness is a total win for you on all levels. If you notice your thoughts are negative, you can make changes that help you feel better. If you notice your feelings are all over the place, you can make changes that help you feel better. If you notice your social life feels stressful, you can practice self-awareness to get a sense of how you play a part—then make changes that help you feel better!

Life *sometimes* gets better by itself, but it *always* gets better when you take an active part. Awareness gives you the power to notice and change habits that trigger anxiety. It helps you feel less like a victim and more like a boss.

Self-Awareness Grows as You Grow

At ages twelve, thirteen, and fourteen, it's easy to feel like the victim of outside authority and circumstances. That's completely normal and understandable. Tweens and young teens often *don't* have a lot of power, and so when things get hard it's easy to blame people and factors outside yourself. It can be challenging to see your part and focus on owning and changing your piece of a bigger picture. If *you* are a tween or young teen, be patient because as you get older, self-awareness will come more easily to you.

Noodle This: You can start practicing self-awareness at any age by noticing situations that really upset you. Instead of getting swept up in intense emotions that cascade into anxiety, push the pause button and try shifting into reporter mode. Focus on the information you note with your five senses: seeing, hearing, smelling, tasting, and touching. Whatever's relevant. Nothing but the facts and direct observations: I see …, I hear …, and so on. Literally picture yourself as a reporter for local news describing a situation.

As girls get older, often fifteen or sixteen and up, they naturally begin to observe their thoughts and feelings with more interest. It's also at this stage that they become more interested in seeing things from different points of view, not just their own.

Self-awareness is something you can work on throughout your life. People who are great at it are so refreshing and easy to be close to because you can say, "Hey, it feels like you've been distracted lately," and they say, "Yes, I can see your point. I *have* been distracted and I'll work on it!"

When you're self-aware, you tend to be less fragile about feedback because you're in a habit of noticing yourself in an honest, realistic way. Self-aware people tend to be more honest and brave and accountable in all those ways that make them awesome friends. You can be that and offer that to all your relationships. The key is to practice observing yourself in a rational way—while also staying open, curious, and kind to yourself and others. Here's how it helped Brynn, age 15:

> I noticed that the mood of my best friend had the power to make or break my day. When her mood was good, my mood

was good. When she was in a bad mood, I'd feel anxious and awkward all day. It just felt like I couldn't be okay unless she was.

Brynn's ability to observe herself was very helpful to her. Once she got clear on what she was observing, she explored the thoughts she often had when she noted her friend's bad mood.

I could literally read her mood within a minute of seeing her. I realized my automatic thought was Oh no, this day is going to suck. Then my mood would sink, and I'd be anxious the rest of the day.

By practicing self-awareness, Brynn made some changes to her thoughts and her choices. Instead of the automatic *Oh no* thought, she intentionally practiced a better thought: *I'll ask if I can help and if I can't, I'll give her space and protect my own mood by hanging out with other people.*

Notice that Brynn didn't get into a bunch of negative thinking about her friend, nor did she start beating up on herself in any way. She objectively noted that her friend's bad mood served as a trigger for her anxiety, and with that information she made a better choice for herself.

Pen Power: Hopefully you're already doing some journaling. If you haven't started yet, now is a perfect time. If you don't want to put your deepest secrets in your journal because you're afraid it will be read by others, no problem. Don't put your deepest secrets in there, but do try to capture observations about yourself and write them down. If you write even one self-observation a day, it will help you grow your self-awareness.

Stasia, age 17: My sister read my journal so I keep a journal on my phone where no one can access it but me. When I write down my feelings, it feels easier to let them go and move on. I feel productive, like I processed them.

Andie, age 17: It's freeing to realize a lot of my thoughts are total garbage. I know myself better now, so when I think a really mean or critical thought about myself or whatever my focus is, I take a step back before letting my thoughts blow me up. I usually give myself a break from thinking about it, do something else, and go back to it later when I feel calmer. Then I can really see things for what they are.

THINKING MISTAKES

Cognitive distortions are another way to refer to thinking mistakes. The term comes from cognitive behavioral therapy (CBT), which is a type of therapy that focuses on alleviating anxiety and depression through monitoring and changing thinking mistakes, aka *stinking thinking*. In a nutshell, CBT asserts that changing your thoughts helps you decrease anxiety and improve your mood.

If you were to interview one hundred young women who have overcome anxiety, you would hear one hundred stories about how those women learned to think differently. You would hear how thinking better leads to feeling better, which leads to more confidence, which leads to saying yes more often, which leads to living life more fully, which leads to feeling more fulfilled and happy!

All these good things work together and feed off each other, so that when you have a relapse moment of negative thinking, you catch it and redirect yourself faster. Let's get started!

Generalizing

Generalizing is when you act as if one incident applies to all similar situations. For example, you have a little crush on someone but then become anxious and convinced your feelings won't be returned. There's no actual evidence for your conviction, but since you had a disappointing crush experience in your past, you assume this too will go badly. Or you have a test in chem that you're sure you're going to bomb. Why? Because the last chem test was a nightmare.

You aren't really considering the crush or the test in a fresh way, in the here and now. You're painting the present with negativity left over from your past disappointment. Can you just see the fat boo-boo in that kind of thinking?

Of course, generalizing is going to make you feel anxious and defeated. Anxious feelings are the opposite of the confidence you'd like to feel entering any potentially stressful situation. To break it down further, your thinking mistake provoked a bunch of feelings. These feelings then influenced your choices about how to act—or not act.

Claire, age 18: I used to think that generalizing was protecting me from getting disappointed and I did it all the time—but I was also negative all the time—and still anxious! My friends called me a pessimist and I realized they were right. I really didn't want to be that person so I started to work on it.

Claire nails it when she notes that her negative thinking habit contained a seed of positive intention: She *felt like* she was protecting herself by anticipating failure and avoiding risk. Instead she was trapping herself in negativity, low confidence, and avoidance behaviors.

Noodle This: Now that you're aware of this easy-to-make thinking mistake, check it out in your own life. If you catch yourself generalizing, gently redirect your thoughts in a more positive direction.

Ask yourself if there is any fresh, relevant information you can pay attention to that will help you see things for what they are. For example: *This crush is a different person and I will pay attention to what I observe instead of what I fear*, or *I studied more for this chem test and I'm better prepared.*

If you're compelled to ponder the previous crush or test, no problem. Do so in a helpful, productive way: *My last crush (or test) didn't go so well. What have I learned from that experience, and since that experience, that could help me out now?*

Feel the difference? You may not be able to stop negative thoughts, but you can definitely learn to observe them and redirect them before they boss you out of living your life. When you guide thoughts in a productive way, you stay engaged with life and reasonable risks. You also gain an opportunity to give yourself credit for learning and growing from previous experiences.

Mind Reading

Mind reading is when a person supposedly knows what another person is thinking without any evidence that the assumptions are true. For example:

- *Whenever people whisper around me, I assume they're talking about me.*

- *I wanted to ask my teacher for an extension but she'd just say no.*

- *I think my friend is annoyed at me.*

In each of these examples, there is no evidence that the thoughts are true. The girls who shared their experiences *assumed* they knew what was going on in the minds of other people. That thinking mistake—not reality—triggered feelings of anxiety.

When you think about the way this works, it's pretty amazing. It's not the whispering that triggered anxiety; it's not the teacher denying the extension, nor is it the potentially annoyed friend. The real problem and the true trigger for anxiety in all the examples is the *mind reading* mistake that each girl made. Who knows what the reality of each situation actually was? Anxiety affected each girl so much that there was no exploration of actual truth.

The sad news about thinking errors is that they create a lot of suffering for no good reason. The good news is that a great deal of the time, reality is better than you think!

Let's look at another cognitive culprit …

Filtering

Filtering is when you eliminate (filter out) positive aspects of a situation and magnify real or imagined negative aspects. For example:

- *I think I bombed the SAT. There were some math questions on there I haven't even learned yet.*

- *I played so badly in the volleyball game. I'm so embarrassed.*

- *Everyone in my class gets what's going on except for me. I don't understand anything.*

In these examples, each girl magnified negative details and filtered out positive aspects of the situation. In the SAT example, the teen who shared was able to take a step back once she realized she was filtering.

She gave herself a chance to calm down and practiced self-care by taking a long shower and a nap.

After her nap, this girl thought more about the test. Her emotions settled down with her self-care, and she identified lots of details that expanded her ability to evaluate her test experience more rationally and realistically. There were many questions and even sections that she felt good about. She still felt bummed about the math questions she couldn't even begin to understand, but in looking at the test experience overall, she arrived at a more realistic evaluation.

In the second and third examples, the girls magnified the negative and filtered out the positive. After a little time and self-care, the volleyball player was able to acknowledge that she had made some good shots and overall had a better game than she initially gave herself credit for. She also identified areas of her play that she wanted to really work hard on before the next game. Similarly, the girl who felt convinced that she was the only one in class who didn't understand what was being taught later realized she was filtering out comments and even audible groaning that she'd heard from her fellow classmates, some of whom were also clearly struggling.

Because these girls were all working to improve their negative thinking habits, they were able to recognize their mistakes and remove the filter from their thinking. Realistic thinking helped each girl feel more powerful and more positive.

Notice that changing thoughts doesn't mean you have to pretend everything is sunshine and unicorns. You don't need to change every negative thought into a positive one. That's too simplistic and superficial—plus you wouldn't believe it anyway. Your goal is to change negative thoughts into rational and realistic thoughts.

The goal in catching your thinking mistakes is to scrub and exfoliate magnified and unnecessary negativity so you can practice seeing yourself and your life more realistically. Realistically, life isn't always the way you'd like it to be. It's the nature of life and you can handle challenges as they come up. Even hard things are easier to face when you look at them as they really are.

On to the next thinking mistake ...

Catastrophizing

Catastrophizing is when you imagine the worst possible outcome of something. Like most cognitive distortions, it creates fear, dread, and lots of anxiety. For example:

- *I'm the most awkward person here.*

- *I'm so raging mad, I'll never get over this.*

- *I made a complete ass out of myself—I'm dying!*

Any of these examples ring a bell for you? If so, great; you have plenty to work on. Just imagine if you were doing everything perfectly and still suffered anxiety. It would mean there's no hope. Fortunately, there's lots you get to change and with every modification you become *more* powerful and anxiety becomes *less* powerful.

Catastrophizing is a kind of dramatizing you probably do from time to time. Some girls say it helps them to *go big* with this kind of emotional expression because they're able to passionately express their most intense thoughts and feelings. If you enjoy an occasional dramatic expression, be careful. Keep self-awareness on board, and pause before getting too sucked into your own surge of dramatic thinking.

Once you've given in to a little drama (and the "catastrophe" of the moment), reset your thinking and come up with replacement thoughts that are more rational, realistic, and helpful, like these:

- *I am not transparent, and just because I think I'm awkward doesn't mean everyone else sees me that way. Other people here probably feel awkward too. I choose to move through this and not take it too seriously.*

- *I'm mad and not thinking rationally. I'm going to practice some self-care so I can turn my emotions down, and I'll go back to this issue later when I've cooled off.*

- *That wasn't my best moment, but I'm probably making it out to be worse than it really was.*

Pen Power: To help you rework your catastrophic thoughts into more realistic ones, write your thoughts down. Doing that helps you (a) move the thought out of your head and onto the paper, and (b) get a new perspective by reading it.

Noodle This: When you step away from a thinking mistake, you give your brain a chance to settle down and reset. Kind of like powering off your phone, glitches go away once you unplug for a bit. During your break, practice self-care to speed up feeling better. Even a cup of tea, a snack, or a walk around the block qualifies as self-care, so no excuses.

Be good to yourself; it helps you think better! Next thinking mistake …

Personalizing

Personalizing is when you take responsibility for something that isn't your fault or react to something by thinking it's about you. Some examples:

- *When a game doesn't go well, I blame myself even though I'm part of a team.*

- *If I see something on social media that I didn't get invited to, I feel horrible about myself.*

- *I feel like people are mad at me a lot. I usually find out they're not.*

Personalizing is exhausting because you implicate yourself as "wrong" and then feel all those feelings, when in reality it's not about you. It's a very common thinking mistake teen girls make because in their desire to feel liked and accepted, they're vulnerable to assuming the worst.

On top of wanting people to like you and be happy with you, you probably hate conflict. You'd probably rather clean the kitchen than have to process a conflict with someone important in your life. No wonder personalizing triggers so much anxiety.

Noodle This: Next time you find yourself personalizing, catch yourself and simply flip your thinking like you'd flip a pancake. For example:

- What if my teammates are mad at me? *What if they're not?* (Ponder this possibility in detail. Notice how it makes you feel.)

- What if I didn't get included because they don't like me? *What if I just didn't get included—and it's not personal.* (Again, ponder and really practice thinking the better thought—it's often more accurate.)

- What if my friend is in a bad mood because of me? *What if she's in a bad mood because of some other stressor? If she's mad at me, I trust her to bring it up. Until then, I won't make that assumption.* (It's great practice to start giving responsibility to other people when it comes to communicating with you. If someone has an issue with you, they can bring it up. Otherwise, drop it.)

When you flip your thinking, make sure to really embrace the new and improved thought. Really feel the relief it brings you, and then commit to sustaining your improved way of thinking and feeling. Practicing thought flipping saves you from sinking into a terrible mood.

Nerd Alert: Thought flipping improves *cognitive flexibility*, which refers to the ability to see a situation from more than one perspective. Cognitive flexibility is an excellent ability and a sign of high emotional intelligence. Next thinking mistake …

Emotional Reasoning

Emotional reasoning is a thought process by which emotions mistakenly tell you that something is true even when there is evidence that it is not. Examples of thinking mistakes based on emotional reasoning:

- *I feel like a failure; therefore I am a failure.*

- *I feel disgusting and ugly; therefore I'm right and that's how others see me.*

- *I feel less intelligent than other people in this class; therefore I am.*

If you mistake your thoughts and feelings for facts, you're committing the emotional reasoning error. You probably don't include a "therefore" in your thinking like the examples because thoughts don't usually present themselves that clearly and articulately. It's more like you get an idea in your head and just accept that it's true, without realizing you're factualizing thoughts.

The worst part about emotional reasoning is that you assume your thoughts are correct and then make decisions based on the negative thoughts. Tragedy! You're avoiding opportunities in order to avoid risks and dangers that don't even exist.

The truth about thoughts is that you have thousands of them a day and many of them are totally random, irrational, or just plain wrong, wrong, wrong. Begin to call out and throw out your irrational, unrealistic, and troublemaking thoughts.

Wrapping Up Thinking Mistakes

As you begin to notice and write down your cognitive distortions, you'll notice some of your thoughts contain more than one thinking mistake. For example: *I played terribly today, and I know my coach is pissed* contains a filtering error, a mind-reading mistake, and a personalizing boo-boo. Three in one! That's okay, because thinking mistakes often tangle together, and as you learn to spot them, untangling gets easier and easier. If you'd like to learn about other types of thinking mistakes, search "cognitive distortions" on the internet. There's a lot of info about them.

SELF-TALK

Self-talk is the way you talk to yourself, and it is a reflection of the thoughts you think. If you tend to be encouraging to yourself when you're having a hard time, your self-talk will be positive and kind:

I've got this, I can do it. It's a little scary and I'm uncomfortable but discomfort doesn't mean run and hide. It's an opportunity to be brave and move forward ... yep, I can do this!

Likewise, if you tend to be hard on yourself, your self-talk will be critical and unkind:

I know I'm going to embarrass myself. I'm going to do or say something stupid, and this is going to be a failure.

In order to become more confident and less anxious, you need to identify and replace negative self-talk with encouraging self-talk.

Madi, age 16: Middle school was bad for me. I was bullied by girls I thought were my friends until they dumped me and spread rumors about me. It was so bad that I started this weird habit of thinking even worse things about myself than they could say about me. I told myself that I was fat, ugly, stupid ... those were my go-to's but there were more. I think it gave me power, or I thought it did, but I got depressed and avoided almost everything that had to do with being around people, other than my family.

In therapy, I learned about negative thinking patterns and self-talk. At first it felt impossible to make changes, but I started off by just writing down negative thoughts when they came into my mind. There's something about seeing what you say to yourself on paper. It made me feel genuinely sad for myself—probably for the first time ever. Not only did I deal with outside bullying, now I was dealing with inside bullying because the way I talked to myself was brutal. Once I really could see how I was hating on myself, I made changes.

My life as a sophomore in high school is so much better, and I have real friends now. I sometimes point out their thinking mistakes to them, like personalizing or filtering, and we all try to support each other to stay positive about ourselves and life.

Noodle This: As a self-reflection exercise, review your self-talk habits. Do you say encouraging things to yourself, or are you more likely to be internally critical? If you want to deeply grasp the difference, think about someone you love and how you would support that person if they were going through something stressful. You would of course try your best to be kind and encouraging.

With practice, encouraging self-talk will become your new normal, and since you're starving anxiety of its food supply, it will become weaker and weaker until you catch only glimpses of it pathetically trying to get in on your new and improved life.

Bye-bye horse poop, bye-bye barn flies!

Meet and Greet All Your Feelings

Meet and greet all your feelings as they come and go.

—L. Hemmen

Imagine what life would be like if you could really let feelings come and go, like guests or visitors. Instead of feeling ambushed and held hostage by intense feelings, you'd be like, *Hello Contentment, come on in and stay awhile*, or *Oh, hey Impatience … hey Irritability. You guys are hanging out a lot together lately. I need to do some self-reflecting to figure out why.*

Learning to befriend and work with all your feelings, also called emotions, helps you build the best relationship possible with yourself. The better you are with *you*, the less anxiety knocks at your door. When it comes to befriending and working with feelings, you may have room for improvement.

Cate, age 17: I wouldn't say I have a good relationship with my emotions, no. I would say they overwhelm me and control my mood a lot.

Simone, age 14: I'm so scared of feeling anxious that I just try to shut out all my feelings. I'm a master distractor.

Sierra, age 17: Ummmm. I'm good with the good feelings, obviously. I try to ignore the bad ones. (Interviewer: Does that work?) Nope. Not really. (Laughing)

Getting overwhelmed by feelings is natural when you don't know how to meet them as visitors. Avoidance techniques make sense when you don't have better alternatives. Unfortunately, avoiding feelings by shutting them down, ignoring them, rejecting them, burying them, numbing them, or distracting just doesn't work. If it did, this tip would be called "Hit and Quit All Your Feelings." It would! But that's not the plan because all your visitors have a purpose and deserve your respect.

THE FEEL DEAL

Some people say there are eight basic emotions, followed by tons of variations of those basics. The great eight are joy, sadness, fear, disgust, surprise, anticipation, anger, and trust. Each one has a message and serves as a guide for you. Just as physical hunger and sleepiness signal you to meet your body's needs, feelings signal you to pay attention to your emotional needs. Some feelings will require you to take action in order to best care for yourself. Other feelings won't require action other than a moment of acknowledgment and care.

Take anger, for example. It's a passionate desire for something to be different and/or a signal that someone or something is intruding on your boundaries. It activates and guides you to focus and possibly respond to a situation that needs attention.

Anger gets a bad rep because lots of people are unskillful in the actions they take when they're angry. But anger itself is an important emotion. Your challenge is to feel it, decide if there's an action you should take, and be skillful in the execution of the action—for example, "I'm angry that you're flaking on me for your boyfriend again. I need you to follow through with plans we set up. I'm not going to stay angry—just letting you know how I'm feeling."

Joy, on the other hand, motivates you to do more of whatever's fluffing your joy factor—like connecting with someone you like or engaging in a feel-good activity. For example, you switch up your routine so that you get your homework done first and then reward yourself with a bath and some pleasure reading. As you slip into your warm bubbles with your book, you get that happy-dance feeling in your heart and decide this change in routine is working for you.

Guilt helps you take a look at your behavior to see what needs changing. Feeling guilty for making a choice that brings upset to someone guides you to be more considerate in the future. Feeling guilt, even for our ancestors, motivated conscientious behavior choices—which helped us be here today. When you feel guilty, it's an opportunity to self-reflect and decide if something needs changing or if there's something to apologize for.

Every single one of your feelings has survival value, meaning you are wired to feel each one. You're here as a modern-day teenager because every one of your emotions helped the human species survive and evolve. Instead of fighting or denying feelings, life gets so much better when you learn to befriend them and learn how to respond to each one.

POSITIVITY TRAP

You can be a positive person and still feel all your feelings. Sometimes teens want to squash a painful feeling, but that will work against you if you don't first meet and greet that feeling. Forcing positivity can be a way to deny feelings, which just doesn't work because feelings require at least a bit of attention and have a way of popping out messily when stuffed down.

In emotional moments, remind yourself that feelings are neither good nor bad. You don't get an A+ for being happy, nor do you get a F- for being sad, angry, insecure, or anxious. If you're a rich, sensitive, alive human, you'll feel it *all*, so open your mind to meeting and greeting all your feelings before releasing them. When you're ready to move on, self-care is the perfect way to pivot out of a feeling and into a different state of mind.

Befriending feelings helps you become stronger and healthier emotionally, which in turn helps you avoid overwhelming encounters with anxiety.

Noodle This: Imagine encountering all your feelings in a relaxed, accepting way. Imagine cultivating an open, caring attitude toward all your feelings. Most importantly, imagine meeting each one without fear. Feelings aren't facts, they're energy in your body. The better your attitude toward meeting and accepting each one, the better you'll feel about yourself and the opportunities life brings you.

GETTING COMFY WITH EMOTIONS

The better you get at recognizing and naming your emotions, the better you'll be with other people's emotions. Instead of having that awkward moment when someone you care about freaks out, you'll stay calm and relaxed because you'll know that emotions come and go—and mostly just want some attention and care.

You don't have to say anything brilliant when someone you love is upset. You can just be present and caring, like you're learning to be with your own feelings. Getting comfy with emotions is great for your relationships because it allows you to get closer to people—beyond surface level.

Even better, anxiety goes right out the window as you become comfortable with feelings because anxiety feeds on discomfort with human emotion. The more you meet, greet, and release emotions, the more you can keep moving through life without feeling tackled by unfelt feelings and the anxiety they trigger.

NAKED AND AFRAID

There's a saying that anything you hate or reject about yourself turns against you. Rejecting parts of yourself, including uncomfortable feelings, only results in those feelings either withering from lack of care or going rogue only to pop out at an inconvenient time, in an inconvenient way.

That's because ignored feelings are a lot like ignored children. They get noisier and more demanding the longer you neglect them. A few may wander away and descend into hopelessness. (Ignored children often become depressed.) The rest become feral and band together like wild, naked savages marauding through the tangled rain forest of your emotional world—until boom! They get your attention, and it's not pleasant.

As you begin to meet and greet all your naked little savages, learning their names and accepting them without judgment, you'll notice yourself feeling different—in a good way. You'll notice a stronger, kinder connection with all your feelings and you'll experience fewer "boom" moments.

It might sound counterintuitive: *Why get to know the painful feelings? Isn't that just poking the bear?* The answer is no. Since feelings are affecting your thoughts, your mood, and your confidence *all the time*, it actually chills them out when you take time to notice them.

Like noisy children, they settle down with a little acknowledgment. You'll find they start behaving much better, and so will anxiety.

> Mischa, age 17: I was afraid that if I began to give my feelings more interest and attention that all the painful feelings would feel even worse. I have a lot of intense feelings and got used to just pushing them down all the time—it was automatic. Now I'm just like, "Okay, explosion of insecurity, I feel you ... I got you." (Laughing) Then I relax because even if the emotion sucks, I feel a sense of control in knowing what's going on with me.

Noodle This: Take a moment to self-reflect. How are you with your wild, naked savages? Which ones have come to visit lately? How did you respond? There's no right or wrong answer. The goal is to simply become more aware.

There's so much on your radar all day that it's easy to be out of the loop with your own feelings. You're learning to self-reflect, which promotes your growing self-awareness. When you're aware, you can make small changes, so if there's room for improvement, read on for support in becoming a better hostess to all your emotional visitors.

CLASS NOT OFFERED

As a teen, you are subjected to lessons, lectures, feedback, coaching, and teaching moments all day, every day. From parents to teachers to coaches to random strangers, people are teaching you something. With all the instruction, you would think someone would come up with a sensible way to teach you how to have a good relationship with your emotions. Since emotional intelligence is highly predictive of success in life (more than your grades or SAT score), you'd think there would be at least a minute spent on the topic. But this is rarely the case—because most adults haven't learned either. It builds compassionate understanding. No wonder so many people of all ages suffer from anxiety.

If anything, you may hear things like "Don't be so sensitive" or "Calm down," which could *not* be *less* helpful. Tell someone with an anxiety flare-up to just relax and you're likely to receive a withering glare that says, *You really don't get it, do you?*

Feelings are part of what makes you real and human. Reject them and you reject your humanity. Avoidance tactics only flatten out your personality, trigger anxiety, and culminate in uncontrollable emotional eruptions *or*, the opposite, depression.

IF YOU CAN'T BEAT 'EM, MEET 'EM!

Once you notice your feelings, you can begin the meet-and-greet process. Naming feelings simply means knowing the name of the feeling you're experiencing. If your heart just sank when you checked Instagram, pause and see if you can identify exactly what feeling showed up in your body. Maybe it was irritation, insecurity, sadness, jealousy, or resentment.

Naming emotions is huge when it comes to building your emotional intelligence. Start noticing feelings, naming them, sending care, and then releasing them. Check out this list of feelings so you can recognize them when they arrive at your doorstep.

amazed	foolish	peaceful
annoyed	frustrated	proud
angry	furious	relieved
anxious	happy	resentful
ashamed	hopeful	sad
bitter	hurt	satisfied
bored	insecure	scared
comfortable	inspired	self-conscious
confused	irritated	shocked
content	jealous	silly
determined	joyful	suspicious
disdainful	lonely	tense
disgusted	lost	terrified
eager	loving	trapped
embarrassed	miserable	uncomfortable
energetic	motivated	worried
envious	nervous	
excited	overwhelmed	

Pen Power: *Inside-out writing* is a way to write in your anxiety notebook that helps you improve your relationships with your emotions. Every day, scan the emotions list while staying open to your body's sensations. As you read through the list, see if any of the emotions paid a visit to you that day. Often you'll notice your body responding to one or more emotions on the list because your body is where the emotion is experienced. Just be open and curious as you do this exercise. Write a sentence about how the feeling registers in your body (inside) and what triggered the emotion (outside).

> Alex, age 18: I felt confused and irritated this morning. The confusion registered in my head but I felt the irritation all over. I notice irritation really comes out on the people I'm around. The trigger was calc and how hard it is and how frustrated I am with the teacher. I'm trying to just sit with the feelings without sinking down so I'm watching my thoughts too.

In Alex's case, she also noted how the feelings trigger behavior—snappiness—and noting that, she was able to be careful and conscientious around her friends and family.

FROM HOSTAGE TO HOSTESS

When you're a *hostage* to your feelings, it's easy to make sweeping interpretations of your life, such as:

- My life is shi*@!
- Everything is terrible!

- I suck!

- My life sucks!

- My friends suck!

Notice any real emotional information in the above examples? Nope, there isn't any. There are only judgments, and the more stuck you are on the judgments, the less open and caring you are to your emotional visitors. The worst part of getting stuck in harsh judgments such as *My life sucks* is that you end up blocking the meet-and-greet process and you unintentionally trigger anxiety.

When you're *hostess* to your feelings, you meet, greet, and sometimes get info that actually helps; for example, after texting with one friend about another friend, you notice an uncomfortable feeling arising: *Ohhh … that feeling … ugh, it's guilt. I got a little carried away with my venting. Is there anything else? Yeah, I feel anxious—sometimes convos that are meant to be confidential leak out. That's definitely happened before …*

In this example, you can take guidance from the feeling; for example, *I'm going to try to talk less about people behind their backs. Guilt and anxiety are helping me see that I don't like this behavior in myself.*

No need to get harsh with yourself. You're not here to be perfect—you're here to learn and grow, and that's what you're doing. If you weren't, you wouldn't be reading this guide. By befriending the guilty and anxious feelings that were triggered by your behavior, you can make small changes that protect you in the future. This is how working with your feelings can help you be more of your best self—which, in return, removes more anxiety from your life!

TROUBLE WITH NAMES

If you meet a feeling, but can't think of its name and don't know why it's there, don't worry about it. Just notice the sensations in your body; for example, *There's a sinking feeling in my chest. Not sure why.* Then just chill and let yourself feel it for a few moments. Send it care, and move on to self-care or a healthy distraction.

Fun reading, taking a shower (or bath or walk), calling a friend, doing art, listening to music, writing in your journal, making a cup of tea or a healthy snack, organizing something, playing with a pet are just a few choices. Over time, you'll find that you get better at chilling with your feelings and that the names of feelings come to you more easily. Be patient and gentle with yourself.

MEET-AND-GREET SCENARIOS

Your life is busy and you may wonder when you're supposed to squeeze in this whole befriending your feelings concept. Here are three main scenarios that will help you get started.

The Check-In

A couple of times a day, take a few deep breaths and scan inside your body for an emotional check-in.

- Notice how you feel in your heart, your chest area, your belly.

- Ask yourself, *What feels emotionally true for me right now?* or *What feelings want my attention in this moment?*

- Sense how the emotions in your body respond to your gentle questioning. See if you can identify the name of any feeling or feelings you notice; for example, sadness, anger, fear, excitement.

- If your mind naturally gravitates to something that affected you earlier in the day, breathe into any feelings that come up. Literally inhale, allowing any feelings that want your attention to surface. No judging, resisting, or avoiding. Just invite and observe.

- If you don't know the name of the feeling, just notice and sit with the sensations. Is the emotional energy moving or still? If it had a color or shape, what would it be? Trust anything that comes to you. You're simply showing interest and care.

- Ask yourself if there are any other feelings that want your attention. Sometimes more feelings surface, and you can continue noticing and naming. Sometimes, you'll feel complete with just the check-in.

- Go back to your day! Notice how you feel, and don't be surprised if you feel more grounded and peaceful, even if the feelings you noticed were uncomfortable.

Emotional check-ins can be something you tether to a daily activity to help you remember and set up the habit. For example, you can give your emotions a check-in every time you take a shower, or during your ride home from school, or while you sip a cup of soothing tea as you just chill out. Some teens like to have their journal close by to capture insights they have about themselves and their feelings. Next opportunity ...

The Party Crasher

Sometimes a visitor just crashes in on you hard—no emotional check-in necessary. Party crashers are intense feelings that feel like they're exploding inside of you. They can be overwhelming and even scary. Here's how to handle them:

- Take a breath and note that you're feeling an intense emotion. Some teens like to imagine telling their internal therapist about the feeling: *Ugh, I feel hot and nauseous and my heart is thumping out of my chest.*

- See if you can name the feeling—for example, *Oh this feels like a fear bomb going off*—and offer kindness and care to the feeling: *I'm just going to breathe and try to be gentle with myself and this feeling.* You might even remember something you've learned in this guide that can soothe you: *Just because I feel anxiety doesn't mean I'm in actual danger. I'm going to try to relax into the feeling and not let my thoughts run wild.*

- Focus on relaxing your body. It can help to intentionally tense and then relax different muscles, like the ones in your face, your arms, your torso, your legs. As you release each tensed muscle, imagine you're also releasing the tense feeling.

- Soothe with self-talk. Become amazing at talking to yourself with the kindness you would direct to someone you love: *I'm okay in this moment. I'm going to try to slow myself down and remember that with time, I'll be able to think better and feel better.*

- After noticing the feeling, sitting with it, and offering it care and soothing, you may want to help it release by turning your attention to self-care or a healthy distraction.

You can always go back to the feeling later to see if you need to take some kind of action or explore it more through journaling or talking to an emotionally safe person, like a trusted friend or adult. Next opportunity …

The Attention Seeker

Sometimes visitors show up in your behavior as a way to get your attention. For example, your friends ask you what's wrong, your parents call you sassy, your sibling calls you salty, and you realize one of your visitors is affecting your behavior.

When your behavior is out of whack, suspect that a naked savage may be causing trouble. Take a quiet moment with yourself to breathe and do an emotional check-in, as described earlier.

Now you can start playing hostess to all your emotional visitors. No need to become landlord—feelings don't need to move in and eat your last cookie. You simply need to notice, meet, and greet them as they arrive. Once given a little of your caring attention, they usually move along quite nicely on their own.

THE NINETY-SECOND RULE

According to brain researcher Dr. Jill Bolte Taylor, when you're emotionally triggered, it takes less than ninety seconds for the emotion to hit, surge chemically through your bloodstream, and get flushed out. Interesting! If this is true, why do so many uncomfortable feelings get stuck and have the power to ruin an entire day?

After the emotion has flushed through, it's you who decides if you want to continue to keep it alive. Guess how you'd go about doing this? (Hint: Think of Tip 3.) Yep, with your thinking!

Gemma, age 19: All through high school, my best friend got a lot of guy attention, constantly. Wherever we'd go and whatever we'd do, she'd have guys come up to her and chat her up while I was like, Helloooo … am I even here? Every time it happened I'd get a literal stabbing of insecurity and jealousy, then I'd feel like a bad friend and terrible person, then I'd think about how ugly and basically horrible I was.

Gemma's emotional makeover:

One of my first college classes was called Emotional Dynamics. I learned a lot in that class, and it's made me so much better with naming my feelings and letting them go. I still get flare-ups of intense emotions but now I stop myself from getting into a big, hopeless "story" about how pathetic I am. I actually never talk mean to myself for what I feel anymore. I just let myself feel however I do, sit with it awhile to see what I can learn about myself, and then move on.

SOOTHE OR SPIKE

Meeting and greeting your feelings is five-star emotional care. As you can see in Gemma's example, from there you have the power to spike your misery or soothe it. It all depends on how you create a story or interpretation out of your feelings.

For example, let's say you are on social media when—boom! You see a post of your friends doing something you were not informed about. You automatically register uncomfortable feelings in your body. Before your mind begins to race with every possible negative thought, you pause. You tune into your body. You notice.

Your noticing sesh might go something like this: *Ughhh ... I feel bad, bad, bad. Okay, what else? I feel pain, yes, a dropping sensation in my belly. Okay, just notice with openness and care. Breathe, yes, breathing is good. Slow yourself down. Tense and relax a few muscle groups. That feels somewhat better. Is anything else happening? Burning in my throat, as if I could cry. Okay, anything else? Nope, that's it for now.*

Take a few more deep breaths, and let yourself know that in this moment, you are okay. You won't let yourself get caught up in the list of thinking mistakes, nor will you allow fear to create an elaborate rejection story. Instead, you take a break and practice some kind of self-care. Later, you can decide how you want to respond to what upset you.

You may feel the grip of anxiety in your heart, the searing burn of anger, impatience, or jealousy in your chest, or the slow, churning heaviness of sadness in your belly. All emotions register as energy in your body. When they hit you hard, practice pausing, breathing, and noticing.

You're already doing great! The world is full of people who don't know how to do what you're doing now. And it's too bad because befriending your feelings by showing interest in them has many benefits:

- It toggles energy away from thinking, giving your mind a minute to rest. When your mind can rest and reset, thoughts don't run wild like racehorses in the Kentucky Derby.

- It signals your heart, your soul, and your savages that you care. You're showing interest and openness and care to your emotional world. Like any relationship, your connection with your emotional self blossoms when you show you care.

RELEASE AND RESET

Meeting and greeting feelings helps you be your true self without suffocating discomfort. Feeling uncomfortable feelings helps you become better at being uncomfortable, which helps you be less anxious. People who report high levels of anxiety often also talk about how much they detest being uncomfortable. In their efforts to be comfortable all the time, they avoid opportunities and reasonable risk taking.

Over time, you build this relationship that all other parts of your life flow from—so it pays to make it a strong one!

Practice Saying Yes

As I say yes to life, life says yes to me.

—Louise Hay

Let's take a moment to appreciate where you are now. You've learned a lot about anxiety, what it is, and the games it plays. You've learned a lot about self-care and how crucial it is in your trajectory toward health and confidence. You know about thinking mistakes and how to correct them, *and* you know about feelings and how to befriend them so they can come and go more peacefully.

You may also be noticing subtle improvements in the way you're feeling. Journaling and self-reflection are helping you both notice and express yourself. These abilities begin to transfer into social interactions because as you get to know and express yourself better, it magically becomes easier to talk to other people and connect with them. Even simple interactions with strangers feel more natural when you create and maintain a higher degree of connection with yourself.

If you have a day of slacking on your tips, self-care for example, simply steer yourself back to your path. No need to be mean to yourself—

ever. Harshness creates negativity, and negativity feeds anxiety, so be kind (yet firm) steering yourself back.

Now, the win fest continues because Tip 5 is here to take you on a field trip, out of your comfort zone and more fully into your life. It all starts with one simple word: yes.

Makenzie, age 20: When I was in high school, there were so many things I wanted to do. I wanted to make new friends, go to football games and dances, just feel involved. But I was afraid of rejection or embarrassing myself, so I spent most of my free time at home with my parents. To make myself feel better, I pretended that I thought all that stuff was stupid and that I didn't want any of it, but I think I just hid behind that so no one would pressure me. I feel sad about how much I missed out on, and really, for what? To avoid feeling awkward or embarrassed? I ended up avoiding life.

I'm in community college now, and I live at home, but I work a part-time job and am more social. I work with customers at my job so I think I just got used to dealing with people and it made me more confident. I also stopped making excuses for why I couldn't or wouldn't do things and started saying yes to more. Now I make an effort to be friendlier even to random people I encounter during my day, like the coffee-kiosk workers on campus or other students in my classes, even my professors. The thing about staying in your comfort zone is that it's lonely in there and it gets pretty boring.

EXPAND YOUR COMFORT ZONE

Like Makenzie, you have life inside your comfort zone (CZ) and life outside your comfort zone. Inside your CZ are people, places, experiences, and behaviors that don't trigger anxiety. When anxiety flares, it's easy to see your CZ as lifesaving, so you cling to it like a koala to a eucalyptus tree.

And like Makenzie, you may also feel torn because your desire for life beyond your eucalyptus tree gnaws at you persistently. Feeling torn is actually a good sign because it's revealing to you that a part (or parts) of you want more life in your life. Not all of you feels anxious. You also have a curious part and an adventurous part. They may be held back by anxiety, but they're there. If you're already in touch with your curious and adventurous parts, but have a specific fear or phobia, get a sense of the fear part as well as the part of you that feels brave and the part of you that is rebellious or freedom seeking—which are very different from the part of you that holds the fear.

According to psychologist Richard Schwartz, our construction is more similar to a head of garlic than it is to an onion. You know how garlic bulbs have all the nestled little cloves? We have lots of parts inside of us, too, and getting in touch with them helps us get to know them.

Getting in touch with the different parts alive inside of you helps you soften parts that have too much power and empower parts that are worried and afraid.

PERSONALITY PLUS

Speaking of your different parts, have you ever felt like a low-key multiple personality? Not the full-blown scenario portrayed in books and movies, but a less catastrophic version? It's very normal actually. One minute you feel open and confident; the next, you feel flooded with self-doubt. One day, you're large and in charge; the next, a sloth would beat you to literally any productive activity. Sometimes your moods are affected by outside events, other times (Surprise!) they're completely random.

It's natural to experience shifts like this. You not only have different moods and energy levels but also different parts (sometimes called subpersonalities) that make up the whole of who you are. According to Dr. Schwartz, knowing how parts work helps you navigate your life and feel more connected.

For example, you may have an open, curious child inside you who wants to have adventures, go places, and experience new things. You may also have a competitive part that fires up from time to time, or a caretaking part that can be super loving and compassionate. You may have an inner hermit who wants to be away from people and the stimulation of life. And an inner rebel who just doesn't care what other people think.

What about a scared little girl part? Most teen girls (and adult women) can easily identify and relate to this part of themselves. When you feel anxious, this is often the part of you that gets your attention. You may hide it as you move through your day—exhausting. Or, you may protect this part by withdrawing from all things anxiety provoking—depressing. When the scared little girl part is making decisions, it's easy to get stuck in your CZ.

It's a perfect time to become curious and aware of your different parts. Just like befriending your feelings, getting to know and befriend all your parts helps you work with them. For example, if you're going to a social setting and your shy part is shuffled forward and feeling very uncomfortable, you can become aware of that and work with it.

Once you're aware, you can send care to the shy part and tuck her away for a while. When you intentionally breathe into your curious, adventurous self, you can psych yourself up to enter that social situation with a different attitude and energy.

Pen Power: Imagine you're babysitting a precious little girl. Imagine you're walking her into her swimming lesson (or any situation you'd like to imagine). Picture how she's dressed and how her hair is done. Imagine she grips your hand tighter and looks up at you in concern as you approach the pool and the commotion around it. Your heart melts. You feel her vulnerability. You kneel next to her and look into her eyes to offer reassurance. What do you say?

Grab your journal and pour your heart into what you would say to the little girl you're caring for. Keep in mind there's part of this cutie-pie that wants to get into the pool. She wants to explore a new adventure and experience. She just feels overwhelmed and unsure. What do you say to her?

Next time you're leaning into a new experience outside your CZ, talk to the scared little girl inside *you* with as much love, tenderness, and reassurance as you can. Getting good at giving yourself compassionate reassurance helps you breathe bravery into the more vulnerable parts of your being.

LEAD THE FOLLOWER

Finding your yes means you take your scared parts by the hand and walk them gently toward life beyond your CZ. Whether it's becoming more social or making friends with the fact that you share the earth with spiders (who are mostly minding their own business, btw), your tip work is strengthening your core self.

You can think of your core, or deepest, self as your most genuine, soulful, life-loving self. Think of the last time you had a big laugh: that's your core self, large and in charge and loving life.

Your anxious self may take up a little (or a lot) of surface territory, but your deepest self is like a sun that lives in the core of your being. It's the nature of that sun to radiate brightly through your being, outward toward life. Fear is the icy crust that traps it inside, but the stronger and brighter the sun shines with the tip work you're doing, the more you melt the ice.

Your deepest self naturally says yes to life: *yes, I want to go, do, see, have, and be **more**.*

As you practice breathing into your core self, you can play with shuffling your braver parts forward. Have fun with this practice. Fake it 'til you make it is a great motto for you—which doesn't mean you're fake. It just means you're practicing being the you who lives outside your CZ without taking anxiety or fear too seriously.

You may even tap into your ten-year-old self because that's often an age when girls feel passionate about what they want to do—also a time when girls don't care that much what other people think. Hmmmm … interesting how these things go together. Anyway! Your mission is to reclaim your adventurous self, no matter how old she is, because she wants more out of life.

Triggers

The triggers that lie outside your CZ are as unique as you are. You may be a worrier and preoccupied with a fear that "bad things" might happen in the world beyond your comfort zone. Or you may feel anxiety when you don't know exactly what to expect in a situation, so it's hard to make commitments and follow through with them.

You may have a specific phobia about spiders, bees, public speaking, driving, heights, germs, or airplane travel, or even a fear of vomiting. Or an anxious preoccupation with your physical health and safety or the health and safety of the people you love.

Last but definitely not least (the list of triggers for anxiety is endless), you may feel anxious around other teens or in social situations, fearing that other people are evaluating you negatively. As a companion trigger to social anxiety, you may feel uncomfortably overfocused on your appearance or personality, which you evaluate negatively—making it even harder to relax around other people and be your true self.

Many teens have not one but a creative combo of anxieties that bully them. Whether life outside your CZ is full of triggers, or contains just a few ass kickers, the steps toward growth and freedom are the same. Let's start out by taking stock of what you're working with in order to set you up for the anxiety slayers ahead.

Get Artsy

Think of the elements both inside and outside your CZ as inventory. Like all inventory, yours needs to be checked so you can be clear what you have and where you have it.

Grab some crayons or colored pencils or markers. Either in your journal or on a separate piece of paper, draw a circle to represent your CZ. Make your circle big enough to write in.

Inside and outside your circle, list the inventory items that lie inside and outside your CZ. You don't need to get overly detailed, but try to capture the big-ticket items. If school is in your CZ but home is not, put school inside the circle and home on the outside. If your bed, your cat, and your screens are inside your CZ, but school and being around other teens are outside, represent that in this mini art project. Include other significant inventory items both inside and outside your CZ. Now you can see what you're working with.

If you want to, tape it somewhere you can see it regularly, because you'll use it for an upcoming exercise.

> A note from Makenzie: For me this was a reality check because I've already accomplished some big steps outside my comfort zone, so when I listed stuff inside my circle, it felt good that a lot of those things used to be outside my circle—but aren't anymore. I had a moment … (Laughing) I felt proud. And I also realized that there's basically no end to expanding my comfort zone 'cause I want to keep growing and making my life better. And there's always new stuff that I'm going to want to do.

RERAIL YOUR DERAIL

Makenzie's insight that expanding her CZ is a never-ending adventure is spot-on. Human nature has designed you to continue to grow and expand, which in turn sparks new interests, which in turn motivates you to grow and expand some more. Thank goodness, because growth keeps life interesting.

When you were a baby, you worked on grasping things and rolling over. But that wasn't enough for you—not for long. You wanted mobility and figured out you could get yourself from point A to point B by rolling, then scooting, then crawling, then walking. Insatiable!

Soon you took movement for granted and moved on to your next focus. Big-girl undies, among other things. To rock your big-girl undies, you needed to master peeing in the potty—which you eventually crushed, despite initial feelings of trepidation. When you were fiveish, you worked on mastering monkey bars, running fast, coloring inside the lines, and whatever else called to your spirit. Challenging yourself was natural and fun.

Then you hit middle school. Hopefully, middle school wasn't treacherous for you, but if it was, you're not alone. In the transition from little girl to teen, many girls get derailed from following the calling of their spirit to following the calling of external expectations. It's a time when stress seems to come from all directions: parents, teachers, coaches, friends all seem to need something specific from you.

In modern-day culture, there are a whole lot of expectations. Never before, in fact, have teens been under so much pressure. And teen girls, more than boys, feel that pressure and want to meet expectations so they can feel peace, approval, and acceptance from all the people they want to please.

The cost of derailment? Love of life often gets replaced with a fear of not being good enough, hot enough, popular enough, smart enough … you get the picture. No wonder anxiety often intensifies in middle school and high school.

Noodle This: Try to get a sense of the girl inside you who loves life. Reconnect with the part of you that is curious and interested. Try new things or reconnect with things that make you happy and healthy.

An update from Miranda, age 16: Weirdly, this is what I'm most proud of lately. Everyone in my family knows I'm working with my airplane travel issue. I've been doing a lot of work on it, googling stuff, imagining myself on the flight while practicing breathing exercises. I talked to a pilot friend of my dad's. Then, for my birthday, my granny was joking around and said she wanted to buy me roller skates so I could lighten up and remember that I'm still a kid. Here's the funny part: I said, "Yes please!" So yeah, (laughing) I skate now. It's so not a thing to skate in my town, at my age, but I don't care. My cousin goes with me 'cause she's in college and she really doesn't care what anyone thinks, and we can't help but smile and laugh. We mostly find parking lots and low-profile places but we have a blast and it helps me not take myself too seriously.

Do you need a five-year-old moment? Is there anything joyful your inner kindergartener wants to say yes to? If so, saying yes to the curious child inside you not only awakens your spirit's love for life, it warms up your *yes!* for other adventures.

YES! PRACTICE BEGINS NOW

Yes is so much more than the word that goes with nodding your head. It's a head-to-toe physical and emotional experience of bravery, openness, and commitment to living life fully. Don't expect zero anxiety as you start your Yes! practice. Anxiety is often a sign that you are stretching yourself bravely toward growth. Tolerating the anxiety and continuing to move in the desired direction is what it's all about. *The only way out is through.* Here's how to practice:

Choose one of the inventory items. Make it one that's outside your CZ, and without getting tangled in your No, practice saying yes to that thing. Keep it simple and don't overthink because you're just practicing a new attitude. All things that flow from your Yes flow more easily. All things that flow from No, well … they don't actually flow. No is a block.

Chloe, age 16, chose learning to drive: I've been avoiding it but it's getting to the point that my parents are annoyed with me and gave me a deadline, which makes me even more anxious.

Hold the item in your mind. Now close your eyes and inhale deeply into the part of you that *wants* the thing that scares you. Maybe you want it because there are benefits connected to having it, or maybe you want it because resisting it causes issues in your life. Even if 95 percent of you says no, and only 5 percent of you says yes, breathe fully into that 5 percent. Repeat this simple breathing exercise several times.

Chloe: I think about 75 percent of me wants to drive. It's just that the 25 percent of me that's scared is more intense for some reason. Breathing into the 75 percent of me that wants it was weird and interesting because I'm used to giving all my attention to the other 25 percent. (Laughing) I guess that's why it's more intense.

Either silently or aloud, say *yes* to this item. Picture yourself doing the thing you want and generate positive feelings as you picture it. Fake it 'til you make it and have fun with the details. Imagine yourself feeling good, proud, alive, confident. Keep repeating the word *yes*, noticing how it feels in your mind and in your body. End this exercise by raising your arms in a victory pose, like athletes do when they've just done something amazing.

Continue this exercise often. You can do it for one minute or five. You can do it whenever and wherever—it's like taking your Yes to the gym and making it stronger. Have fun with Yes practice and get good at it because guess what you're doing? Yep, you're rewiring your brain because you're practicing a new habit. Yes practice for fun leads to a Yes answer IRL, so get to it!

Chloe chose driving because it's her biggest concern. Miranda's been working on airplane travel because it's most important to her. What do you choose?

Nerd Alert: When you feel the tingles of fear and anxiety, your nervous system and brain alarm are wondering if they should ramp up to respond to danger. To help adjust and reset your alarm, try telling yourself that you're actually *excited*. The physical signs are similar, and research shows recasting anxiety as excitement is helpful.

Start Your Yes! Challenge

As promised, all your tips are based on baby steps in the direction of growth and expansion. Building your confidence, knowledge, and affect tolerance helps you build bravery and the ability to sustain positive momentum.

Nerd Alert: *Affect tolerance* is a psychological term that refers to the ability to bear (tolerate) your own affect (feelings). For example, when you say yes, even though you fear feeling uncomfortable or awkward, you become more tolerant of these uncomfortable feelings. Feeling fear and moving ahead anyway is an example of strong affect tolerance.

It's human nature to recoil from fear as a way of rejecting (not tolerating) the trigger. When your fears aren't actually dangerous, you are much better off practicing your yes, tolerating the fear, and moving bravely toward, toward, toward that which you fear.

You may even have the famous teen girl talent for resisting and saying *no!* with so much intensity and conviction that the people in your life mistake you for a fire-breathing dragon and back off. It's a short-term win, but is it really?

In the little picture, saying no brings you relief, but in the bigger picture, you're not growing. You don't have to say yes to everything, but when you know you're avoiding something that the deeper (and braver) you actually wants to do or needs to do, you probably need to say yes.

Yes doesn't mean you're not scared. It doesn't mean you're totally confident. It means you are scared, anxious, or uncomfortable *but you're moving forward anyway*. It means you are tapping into the brave beast that you are capable of being, and it means you are saying yes to your life, your growth, and your freedom from being bullied by anxiety.

Warm Up Your Yes

As a warm-up, picture your inventory item and repeat the following:

- Yes, I will try.

- Yes, I can take one step at a time and move toward things that help me grow.

- Yes, I can do this.

- Yes, I can tolerate my discomfort as I move forward.

- Yes, I've got this.

- Yes, I can feel fear, tolerate that feeling, and keep moving forward.

- Yes, yes, yes, yes.

Okay! You're ready to ...

Say Yes to Liking Yourself

If you are hard on yourself, self-critical, and more focused on what's "wrong" with you than what's right—it's time to just stop. No good comes from you not liking yourself so just say yes to liking yourself. Don't wait until you're perfect; don't wait for anything. Like yourself now, no matter what.

If it's a good day, like yourself. If it's a bad day, like yourself even more. If you want to make changes in your life, it's especially important to come from a place of liking yourself because when you hate yourself into changing, it just doesn't work.

Anything you hate about yourself gets worse. If you want to make changes, love is the best motivator.

So you might as well say yes to liking yourself, caring for yourself, and being patient with yourself, because everything in your life works better when you do.

Say Yes to Feeling Uncomfortable

Anxiety has a way of making teen girls extremely tuned into any and all signs of discomfort. First day of school? You suddenly become excruciatingly concerned with any signs of your emotional or physical discomfort. New situation or healthy risk? You find yourself focusing on what your stomach is doing, how you look, what you're afraid could go wrong.

It's like having a twenty-four-hour guard on duty, scouting for signs of discomfort. Of course, anytime your scout is on duty, you're bound to find something to focus on. Once your focus gets locked, whatever you're paying attention to gets bigger and bigger. Yikes, no wonder you want to scamper back to your CZ.

Of course, you never have to say yes to anything that is objectively dangerous or unsafe for your body, mind, or soul. Self-care absolutely includes saying a clear and strong *No* to anything that has a solid risk of causing you harm. It should be stated, however, that situations in which you may be uncomfortable, awkward, or unsure *do not* necessarily qualify as dangerous or unsafe.

Next time you feel discomfort, simply make a note to self in your mind: *hmmm … this is discomfort that I'm feeling.* Then, remind yourself that discomfort is a sign that you're outside your CZ, growing and brave-beasting your way into a bigger life.

Nerd Alert: The way you use language has an impact on how you feel. Notice the difference in how you feel when you note to yourself *This is* *anxiety* or *This is discomfort* instead of *I am anxious* or *I am uncomfortable.* Saying to yourself that you *are* anxious makes it sound like anxious is *who* you are instead of *what* you're experiencing. Anxiety is an experience, not an identity.

Bravery is feeling the discomfort of fear, and moving forward anyway.

Say Yes to Being Imperfect

If you are a perfectionist, even if just in a few areas of your life, say yes to imperfection. Say yes to growing and learning and making mistakes and figuring things out. Say yes to making certain mistakes over and over again before figuring things out.

The more you practice liking yourself, the easier it is to let go of trying to be perfect, and vice versa. Striving for perfection is an endless and loveless venture that will burn you out and suck the honey from your soul. There is no "there" there … it's a miserable, interminable mission to make yourself into someone who can't be criticized or rejected—and it doesn't even work. You don't have to be perfect to deserve your own respect or the respect of others.

Saying yes to being real and imperfect doesn't mean you can't do your best and kick some ass. It just means that you do your best because it feels good to do your best. It just means your best is driven by the passion of your internal sun and not the icy crust of fear that you're not good enough unless you're perfect.

Drop perfectionism like a bad habit because that's exactly what it is. If you do your reasonable best and things don't work out the way you wanted, focus on what you learned from the process.

Just ask any senior with an insanely high GPA who did *not* get into their college of choice whether you can control outcomes. You can't. Focus on what you can control and be reasonable, not ruthless. Most of all, say yes to imperfection in yourself, in others, in outcomes, and in life.

If you are a perfectionist, this is your mantra: *I'm not here to be perfect. I'm here to be real.*

Say Yes to Random Acts of Bravery

Allie, age 14, stumbled upon the power of random acts of bravery when she was at summer camp. Labeling herself as shy, Allie typically avoided volunteering for anything, yet out of the blue, she volunteered to organize her cabin's talent show skit. It meant taking the lead in generating ideas, creating skits, and collaborating with all her cabinmates. She shares:

> I don't know what got into me but I put my hand up before I could think myself out of it. Something in me knew I could do it and it was super fun. I got a lot of props from everybody at the big end-of-camp celebration after the show and I felt proud of myself.

Random acts of bravery can be anything that's safe and a stretch for you. Even little stretches count, like calling the dentist to make an appointment instead of letting a parent do it—if that would be a stretch for you. Or going into the store to buy tampons instead of waiting in the car while your mom does it. The trick is to say yes before no pops out of your mouth. Then, just keep moving toward execution.

Say Yes to Being Happy

It's not uncommon for teen girls to admit that part of them wants to stay miserable. And it's not as crazy as it sounds. Being miserable can become an identity that's scary to give up, especially if you're dealing with something difficult in your life, like a loss or trauma. You may feel stuck in "honoring" your loss or trauma with your misery—as a way of saying it's important and should not be forgotten. Additionally, there are "perks" that go with being miserable.

> Kyla, age 17: I got used to the idea of having depression and anxiety, and I fell into using it as a way of dipping out on everything that stressed me out. Didn't have to drive, get a part-time job, study for the SATs, because I was too fragile. No pressure from anyone and instead everyone else was stressed about me. It gave me a break from all the pressure I felt.

Kyla worked hard at finding her yes for baby steps out of her CZ, which led to bigger and bigger steps, which led to feeling reconnected with life, which led to saying yes to happiness.

Tame Your Tech Time

*Almost everything will work again if you unplug it for
a few minutes, including you.*

—Anne Lamott

At the beginning of this guide, you learned that anxiety isn't something you can pull like a weed. It's not something that gets neatly extracted from your life with one good yank. It would be amazing if that were the case, but since it's not, you're making tons of tiny tweaks that not only help you with anxiety but also help you be the most badass version of yourself in all areas of your life.

In the spirit of *e-x-p-a-n-d-i-n-g* your feel-good, it's time to talk about a force in your life that has a lot of power over the way you feel: screen time.

Okay, so spoiler alert, this is not your favorite topic. You're bored of it and why wouldn't you be? You didn't invent the candy store of devices, apps, and platforms abounding—that came from the adult world. And yet they just won't shut up about your use of them.

Do any of the following admonishments sound familiar?

- Put your phone away. Now!

- Put your phone away or I'll take it.

- You're stuck on your screen again?!?

- Get *off* that device and come be with us!

- Don't you dare be on your phone when company gets here.

- Who are you texting?

- What do you *do* on your phone anyway? Are you sexting?!

- I'm going to throw that device out the window!

To make matters more annoying, adults often have screen issues of their own: *Umm ... hello ... What about you on your phone? Oh, it's okay for you because it's for work? Well, me too! I'm on it for school!* (And let's be honest, maybe you are ... and maybe you aren't.)

Adult nagging, begging, or threatening is as tedious as it is ineffective. Why? Because there are a million ways you can get around finger-wagging adults—and you know them all. The teen girl special? Outlast them! No one can wear down an adult like a motivated teen girl protecting her habits. Screens are addictive enough to really, really motivate you.

As you know, most adults don't really *know* how to get you off your devices. It's like being a lifeguard when you don't know how to swim very well. Without a clear understanding of what you're doing, most parents of teens admit to inconsistent outbursts and intermittent lectures—before giving up.

Despite outbursts about your tech use, you likely get plenty of time to scroll, text, binge watch, and space out on your multiple devices. By continuing to tend to your accounts with the commitment of a lion to her cub, a fatigue factor sets in with the adults in your life, and you "win," but do you really?

DESIGNED TO ADDICT

The addictive seduction of screens is not accidental. Tech companies spend multimillions of dollars on making their platforms and devices as addictive as possible, so you find yourself scrolling scrolling scrolling, watching watching watching. It's not that you're weak! There are many built-in hooks designed to keep you locked on.

For example, they know human nature is to want to get to the bottom, so they designed scrolling content to be bottomless. They know that when you're done bingeing on one show, you feel a little lost—until you see the teaser to a new suggested show and get tipped right into watching it. The more of your time (and your life) they get, the more money for them.

Nerd Alert: Social psychologist Adam Alter, points out a lack of stopping cues as a big reason people have a hard time regulating their screen time. Because the content is designed to capture as much of your time as possible, it's built to be "bottomless," which makes it hard to stop scrolling, playing, and pushing "next episode."

Since teen tech use creates *huge* dollars for tech companies, they're well motivated to keep you hooked, continually coming up with ideas. Just one example: Snapchat streaks. Genius. It feels like a "fail" if you lose your streak.

A win for Snapchat, but is it a win for you? It's a manipulation of your use to entice you into spending more time on the app. It's a false win for you because even though your brain gets a little hit of the feel-good brain chemical dopamine, the high is short and leads to a feeling of hollowness, which is a word often used by teen girls to describe the effects of social media on their mood state.

Another manipulation: an alert letting you know how much time you've been on your phone. Make no mistake about the intent behind this small effort. It's to present a *weensy* bit of "evidence" that tech companies are making an effort. If they don't seem to be responding to public concern over phone use, they face potentially bigger problems in the future. Some other company will come along and appear to be more concerned about the consumer, thereby posing a threat to a company that doesn't seem to care. Tech companies are smart and savvy and playing the "long game." If it helps their "look good" to appear caring, they'll make a show of it, but they are Big Business and their #1 priority is money.

There's even a trend among Silicon Valley tech titans to send *their own kids* to schools that strictly limit screen time and access. Wh-a-a-at? They produce goodies but protect their own kids from using them? This suggests that the who's who in tech companies acknowledge the possibility of negative impacts when it comes to their own kids but are motivated to hit productivity numbers when it comes to you.

Nerd Alert: TED Talks are a great way to expose yourself to new and interesting ideas—you'll find these two on screen time interesting with plenty of thought-provoking ideas to noodle:

- Tristan Harris—"How a Handful of Tech Companies Control Billions of Minds Every Day"

- Adam Alter—"Why Our Screens Make Us Less Happy"

Noodle This: Take a moment to get a sense of your personal relationship with tech use. Take a few breaths, close your eyes, and have a moment of self-reflection, making sure to notice the feelings that come up for you.

Maybe you're not much of a social media girl but you spend hours watching shows or gaming. Maybe you never game but find the minutes melt into hours on YouTube. Maybe, like a lot of teens, you feel a combo of eye lock and dread as you catch up on Instagram stories. As you self-reflect and self-assess, acknowledge both your interest in decreasing your screen use *and* the resistance you have. Both are natural and understandable.

A SCREEN FULL OF ANXIETY

With tech goodies here to stay and growing exponentially in their offerings, you may feel little interest in taming your use. While resistance is understandable, it turns out nagging adults have your best interest in mind.

In survey after survey, screen time is linked with all the things grown-ups want to protect you from. Big things, such as depression, loneliness, unhappiness, low self-esteem, and anxiety. Interestingly, most teen girls have no problem believing research results because they recognize the negative effects of their screen time.

Quinn, age 17: Oh yeah, there's no doubt that social media makes me feel like #@$*. I know rationally what people post is not necessarily reality, but it still makes me feel like my life isn't good enough, and that I'm not good enough. Nothing makes me feel more boring, pathetic, and unattractive than being on social media, but yeah, I still check it several times a day. I spend hours every week on it.

Ava, age 15: I look forward to binge-watching shows whenever I can but I never feel great afterward. I end up snacking a lot, spacing out, and feeling like a blob.

Tate, age 14: I never go on social media and feel better afterward, so yeah, the research doesn't surprise me at all. There are some sites I've cut out, like Tumblr because I was coming across too much dark stuff, but Snapchat is how I communicate with my friends and same with Insta. It's like a love-hate relationship for me.

Lauren, age 17: Nothing is more annoying than hanging out with friends and watching them text other people. (Interviewer: Do you say something about it?) No, because I don't want to be that girl. It's not really acceptable to whine to your friends about it.

Shea, age 17: When I got in trouble recently, my parents took my phone for two weeks. Not gonna lie, I found ways around it—but it was still a massive change in my use. I did not admit this to my parents, but I started feeling much happier a couple of days into my punishment. I mean much happier. I tried to hide it because I didn't want them to keep it longer. (Interviewer: But if you felt better, why would you care if they kept it longer?) Uhh … because I need my phone. You can't have a life without it.

Insight is clearly not the problem for teen girls. You know it's addictive because minutes melt into hours on a regular basis. Then anxiety strikes like a rattlesnake on a field mouse as you realize you haven't started your homework. You've heard the statistic about people checking their phones on average eighty times a day, and you have no problem believing it. Take a breath of willingness to make a few changes that help you downsize the role of screens in your life.

THE REAL DEAL

At this point, there have been massive surveys that look at the effects of social media on teen users. A researcher named Jean Twenge, did an in-depth analysis of *Monitoring the Future*, a huge survey that followed more than a million US eighth, tenth, and twelfth graders. The survey asked students questions about how often they spent time on their phones, tablets, and computers, as well as questions about their IRL social interactions and their overall happiness.

To summarize one of Twenge's conclusions: Pretty much anything you do *on* a screen links strongly to negative emotions, while almost everything you do *off* a screen links with positive emotions. On-screen time includes texting, watching your shows, social media, and the like. Off-screen time includes spending time with friends IRL, participating in sports and exercise, involvement in religious activities, time with family, even time doing homework!

All off-screen time is linked to feeling better, while on-screen time is linked to feeling worse.

She also found that mental health problems sparked like fireworks in 2012, the year when smartphones saturated the US consumer market and over 50 percent of people had a smartphone. *That same year*, mental health problems among teens dramatically increased. *That same year*, more teens reported feeling unhappy, lonely, anxious, depressed, suicidal, and bad about themselves.

Are phones solely responsible for the spike in mental health problems? Probably. Longitudinal research takes time to track and collect, and until more is known, you can bet that phones play a significant role.

Nerd Alert: *Longitudinal research* means that data about the same subjects is collected over a period of time. These studies can span years and even decades.

Turns out social media would be more appropriately named antisocial media since it creates loneliness, not meaningful social connectedness, and causes you to feel bad about yourself.

Special Note: This is not a tip telling you the dangers of sexting or sending nudes to lame asses who ask for them. This is not a tip telling you to be nice online or to report cyberbullying to an adult (after taking screen shots). You very likely know these things because internet conduct and safety is now talked about in schools and in homes.

This is a tip about one thing: giving *less* of your valuable time to screens so that you can build a real life—and a real identity—that brings you real value and less anxiety. In the name of progress toward this goal, read on for tweaks that help.

TINY TECH TWEAKS FOR SUSTAINABLE USE

These five tweaks can take you a long way toward taming your tech time.

Tweak 1: Set Media Time Limits

You don't need the research to know that when it comes to screens, less is better than more. It makes intuitive sense. No one binges on Instagram and feels better afterward. No one falls into the YouTube spiral and comes out feeling refreshed. Realistically, you absolutely can and should trim your use in order to create and protect your well-being.

Sophie, age 16: My anxiety got so bad this last year my mom started taking my phone away. We had huge fights about it before learning about App Limits, which allow me to create a time limit on how long I use social media before alerting me that I've reached my limit. If I want, I can ignore the alert and keep scrolling but I made a firm commitment to my mom and myself to respect the limit and get off. My limit is fifteen minutes, and even though I thought that was totally unrealistic, it turns out it's fine. I'm more focused on what I want to do and I don't get lost. You think you're gonna be socially missing out but really you aren't. (Interviewer: Any change in how you feel?) Oh my God, yes. At first I felt like an addict in withdrawals but now I just feel better and I get sh%# done—and that makes my life less stressful.

Six apps to check out: InMoment, Moment, OffTime, StayOnTask, AppDetox, Space.

Tweak 2: Start Smart

To set yourself up for a good day, tweak your routine by avoiding going on your phone after you turn off your alarm. Going on your phone to check your accounts immediately after waking is like eating an anxiety biscuit smothered in feel-bad, with irritability sprinkles on top. It's just a terrible way to start your day.

Daisy, age 21: For quite a while I noticed myself feeling anxious after checking social media first thing in the morning. I knew it wasn't great for my mind—set but I just did it as a habit and I know so many people my age do. We set alarms on our phones, wake up, turn off our alarms, and our phones are in hand. It feels natural to start checking. I kept getting a little message in my head to get up and do something else—get away from my phone—so finally I did. Now I turn off my alarm and put my phone under my pillow. Then I get up right away and make myself hot water with lemon. I read somewhere that it's great for your digestion, and it makes me feel like I'm making a small effort that sets my day up right. Self—care is very important to me, and creating this routine makes me feel good. I feel my best when I'm on my own side, doing the right things for myself. I hope younger girls try this because it's easy to dismiss feeling bad and act like it's no big deal, but feeling bad is a big deal. Life is challenging and we all deserve to start the day feeling our best.

Tweak 3: Create a DIY Stopping Cue

Emma, age 13: My mom made me watch a few TED Talks with her and yeah, I get it. I know it's all true, that it takes too much of my time for really no value and that it's bad for my mood.

In one of the talks, the guy says to create a stopping cue by choosing everyday things you do and make them your stopping point for being on your phone, like dinner. So now, when my mom says fifteen minutes until dinner, we all turn our phones on silent and put them in a drawer until fifteen minutes after dinner. So now we have some before, during, and after dinner time that is screen-free. At first we would watch the time and run to our phones, but I've noticed we don't do that anymore.

Even though Emma initially assumed her mom's plan for screen-free dinner wouldn't work, she had to admit that it made life better. She noted that her mom was in a much better mood—probably because Emma and her sister now helped out more with dinner and there was less arguing. On her own, Emma decided to extend the idea of DIY stopping cues by creating an additional cue:

I have a lot of trouble falling asleep at night so I decided to make my nighttime routine another stopping cue. Before I wash my face and brush my teeth, I put my phone away for the night. I need to put it in the bottom drawer of the downstairs bathroom so that I can resist the urge—(laughing) luckily I'm too lazy to go get it if I feel weak. Now I read a little before bed or write in my journal or color. There is no doubt it helps with my sleep, and I'm doing it for me, not because anyone is making me.

Noodle This: What can you designate as a stopping cue? Once you've chosen your stopping cue, be impeccable at turning your phone on silent, putting it far away from you, and strictly denying yourself any impulse to "cheat." It's important to have 100 percent integrity with your screen-free time because that way your new habit will wire into your brain as sacred and valued instead of something you're doing half-assed.

Pen Power: Write a sentence or two each day about what you notice about how you feel before, during, and after your screen-free time. Writing will encourage your self-reflection, which encourages your strong, caring, and honest relationship with yourself. You can do it!

Tweak 4: Do a Cleanse

If you're up for doing more than just reducing your tech time, go big and try a cleanse. A tech cleanse means taking a break from one or more of your biggest tech time sucks to explore how it feels. People who do this are amazed with how quickly they feel better. Another win is that you find you fill in the time suck with other activities that actually improve the quality of your life.

In one study, researchers from Stanford University and New York University recruited Facebook users and assigned half the recruits to shut down their accounts for a month. The result? Mood logs kept by all participants showed more happiness in the Facebook-free participants. Wow!

And that's not all: The study also showed that the Facebook-free participants spent more with friends and family. A powerful double win.

Mimi, age 17: I went on an unintentional cleanse last summer when we took a family trip to Indonesia. My parents had me and my brother leave our phones at home. I thought it would be torture to be so disconnected and it was at first. I was surprised at how short it lasted though. For three weeks, I had no phone and just a little contact with friends when I had access to a computer and internet, and not only did I survive, it felt great. It gave me a reality check about what a weird chore social media has become for me. Not even a source of happiness but like a weird responsibility I have to keep up with. When I came home, I made a commitment to change my habits, and I've kept it up for the most part. When I have an occasional binge, I notice how it feels and it's a reminder.

Pen Power: How about doing a cleanse with your friends? Get at least one friend to commit to a weeklong cleanse, or even just a day! In your journal, note how you're feeling and what you're doing in place of your screen time.

Tweak 5: Declutter your phone.

A quick and easy way to calm your addiction to any app is simply to take it off your phone. This is a favorite tip among college-age women who report that out of sight helps distraction stay out of mind.

Tess, age 20: I just keep making tweaks that create distance between me and social media. Not having it on my phone means when I wait in line for something, I look around and stay in the moment instead of staring at my stupid phone. My other tweak is to absolutely make sure I have my "have to's" done before I indulge in screen time. That means my studying, my exercise, my laundry. I'm not willing to get behind in my life because of social media like I did when I was in high school. I can't handle that stress anymore.

Tweak 6: Spend More Time with Friends IRL

Before smartphones saturated the market in 2012, the amount of time teens spent hanging out in person was already on the decline. After 2012, the drop intensified, with teens spending much less time together IRL. The happiest teens, according to one study, are those who are above average in face-to-face social interaction time and below average in social media use.

> Addie, age 14: The research doesn't surprise me at all. I am happiest when I'm with my friends. I even feel better when I'm around random people I don't know, like when I'm out and about downtown or at the mall, or even at the library. It just makes me feel less isolated and in my own head when I'm around other people.

> Lena, age 13: I'm going to try to hang out with friends more. I have two besties, and we're kind of lazy about getting together. We Snapchat constantly but don't actually go anywhere.

TIPS FOR IRL SOCIAL TIME

Since hanging out with friends is good for your mental health, it's time to do more of it. Strive for more "real" connection rather than device-dependent connection in order to explore the benefits for you. Here are some ideas to keep in mind:

Make a clear plan and pitch it to your friends. Often nothing happens socially when no one proposes a concrete plan. Be willing to make a plan that is specific enough to communicate clearly so there's less room for misunderstanding and flaking; for example, *Let's meet at the frozen yogurt place Saturday at noon.*

Set a weekly routine. If you and your friends do something fun, why not make it a weekly routine; for example, *Every Monday, let's meet at Olivia's house and do homework.* It will give you something to look forward to, and if it's already planned, it's easy to keep on your calendar as a consistent commitment.

Get a job. Getting a part-time job works miracles for your confidence—plus, it puts you around other people. Being around other employees is a great way to meet new people, and working with customers gets you out of your own head and into real life! While starting a new job can give you butterflies, you'll soon notice they fly away, leaving you feeling more independent, capable, and confident.

Get physical. Exercise is great for both being around other people and raising confidence and well-being. If you're not one to try out for a school team sport, don't let that stop you. Check out a climbing gym or regular gym, a dance class, a yoga class, Pilates, a martial art—anything that puts you around other people while huffing and puffing.

Look around. Practice more friendliness at school. Since you see the people in your classes regularly, you might as well get to know them. Don't make the mistake of thinking that only your established friends are important to you. Open your mind (and your mouth), and start being chattier, warmer, kinder to the kids right next to you. Small gestures are perfect; for example, *Do you want to see my notes* *from Monday? I noticed you weren't here.* Boom! Kindness and connection—all in one small gesture.

Noodle This: How do you feel when you spend more time with friends and more time exercising? How does that compare with how you feel when you're on your screens? Ultimately, you want the changes you make to come from you, not other people. What do you want to commit to for yourself?

Nerd Alert: Not all screen time is created equal when it comes to negative impact. People who use their phones to check the weather or do a mindfulness practice or store their boarding passes for travel feel great about it.

DON'T BE A PAINFUL POSTER

Hopefully, you're on board for slimming down the time you spend on social media and other screens. When you do indulge, set some guidelines that protect you from going overboard into the sea of endless distraction.

The biggest tip college girls give is that it's best to post infrequently and to post pictures that are more than you looking hot in a selfie. Or in a modeling shoot you're doing with your best friend, taking turns snapping and posing, then evaluating how you look in various settings/outfits/poses. These girls remember their cringey days of spending way too much time creating their social media "look good" personas, while IRL things weren't so great.

Sasha, age 20: Oh, how I cringe when I think about my younger self. I'm all over my little sister making sure she doesn't make the same mistakes, but she's a different kid than I was and doesn't seem to care much about social media. I was obsessed and addicted and—btw—totally anxious all the time. There is such a connection to anxiety and social media. I did a great job making my life look amazing, but it was hollow and lame because I wasn't having an actual life. Now I post rarely and only pictures that reflect something that has actual meaning. When I catch myself getting stuck looking at other people's stuff, I shut it down and do something different. Two minutes later, I feel better. It's a fake world online. You just gotta know that.

Painful posters work hard to get love and approval by focusing more on their online image than on their actual lives. They post a lot of pictures of themselves, often strategically sexualized pics designed to promote themselves as one of the hot girls they follow on Instagram or other apps.

The more pics of yourself you post, the more likely you rate high on a measure called *self-objectification*, which means you think of yourself as an object and see yourself through the eyes of other people who evaluate your worth based on how attractive an object you are.

Stomach turning, huh? You live in a very objectifying culture where girls feel the pressure to be hot and gorgeous. With girls as young as elementary school feeling the pressure to be sexy, it's a sad situation. No surprise that eating disorders, body shame, and food guilt are issues girls who rate high in self-objectification struggle with. And of course, what goes along with all these issues? Anxiety!

Thinking constantly about your weight, your looks, how other people are seeing you, what they're thinking of you is like handcuffing yourself to anxiety. When you notice a preoccupation with what's happening in other people's heads—concerning you—gently walk yourself back into your own experience and ask yourself: *How am I feeling about me right now? What can I do for myself right now, to help me get fully back in my own experience and out of other people's heads?*

You don't need to play to anyone's approval to be valuable. Seeking approval takes you out of your true self, and other people, if anything, judge you negatively for it. There's no upside, so practice noticing and self-correcting.

Ellie, age 22: Don't post that often. Don't show your cleavage, your ass, your abs. It's not powerful. I grew up with the grandma rule that if I wouldn't show a picture to my grandma, I shouldn't post it. I know girls now are saying they post pictures for body positivity, but I think there's a line there because it seems to me they're just putting a new label on something that's still objectification. I know that's a matter of opinion, but I just think we need to get the focus off our bodies being who we are and what we post.

Lily, age 20: If a girl really struggles with anxiety, just get off social media. Seriously, just get off it. It's not as important as you think it is, and you will not miss anything—just superficial junk that means nothing. Work on your real life, on your real self. You will be less anxious that way and I'm speaking from experience.

Now that you're trimming screen time, you're in the perfect position to add a little soul to your life. Tip 7 is ready and waiting to help you reclaim the soulful being you are when not distracted by screen time soul suckage. Life is short and precious—why not spend time creating and supporting the Real You!

Reclaim Your Soulful Self

Put more BE-ing in the Doing.

—Eckhart Tolle

When you were a little girl, you had an easy breezy connection with your soulful self. Life was simpler then because you weren't too concerned with what you *should be* doing or what other people thought of you. You didn't stress about schoolwork, college, love, or climate change. Life wasn't perfect, of course, but even in stressful times you had a magical capacity to enjoy the sweet moments of life.

Little girls are naturally soulful, meaning fully authentic and connected to the magic of life. They take great joy in being in the moment—mind, body, and soul. Need some reminding? Here are just a few examples you may remember:

- floating in pools

- splashing in puddles

- making sand castles

- swinging on monkey bars

- observing caterpillars

- building forts

- climbing trees

- eating the sprinkles off cupcakes—one sprinkle at a time

Little girls are also passionate about *creating* and do so for the sheer pleasure of it. Games, art, stories, music, dance routines, and recipes featuring marshmallows and chocolate chips ... sound familiar?

Tip 7 is here to reconnect you with your soulful self because with all you've got going, there's a good chance you've lost track of her. At a time when being your deepest self isn't exactly what people seem to want from you, you'll find that reconnecting brings a sense of alignment back into your relationship with life.

SEPARATION ANXIETY

Of course, life isn't all coloring books and graham crackers when you're young. Little girls absolutely experience anxious feelings. Fears, however, are usually focused on things *outside* themselves, like monsters or strangers or new situations. It isn't until around middle school that girls begin to experience sharp spikes of fear about themselves and worry about being accepted and keeping up with expectations.

Changes unfold quickly for teens, and in an effort to meet expanding demands, playing with face paint gets replaced with applying makeup. Wearing what's comfy gets replaced with wearing what's trending. Studying caterpillars gets replaced with studying for exams, playdates with texting and social media.

Eager to please all the important people in your life *and* feel good about yourself, you may have started rushing through the pleasures you used to savor. Life is more complicated for teen girls today than it's ever been, which makes it easy to get separated from the *you* who is most essentially *you*: your soulful self.

As the good stuff in life gets scooted over by the stressful stuff, you understandably lose touch with life's small but profound pleasures. Soulfulness gets crowded into a smaller and smaller space, and living in the moment gets replaced with living in your head—lots to do, do, do, and way more to worry about and overthink.

It's probably not a shock to learn that more girls than you might think have huge emotional meltdowns in their teen years. While meltdowns are upsetting for a teen as well as family members, they simply indicate that the teen has more stress than she has internal emotional resources.

When a stressed teen girl does take a break, she's often drawn to screen time instead of soul time. It just seems easier and more compelling. It's at this point in a girl's development that problematic levels of anxiety often move into the picture—taking up the very spot where soulfulness used to live.

Self-care and soul care are the best ways to restock emotional resources. You're already working on self-care—now it's time for soul care.

Then and Now

Remember, anxiety is a naughty little beast and very opportunistic.

Amanda, age 14: I was very confident when I was little.
I probably wasn't a great artist, but I sure thought I was.
I spent hours creating drawings, paintings, playdough

sculptures. (Laughing) At some point, I think I realized I wasn't that good and I stopped doing art.

Hailey, age 16: I loved school up until ninth grade when it became all about grades. Teachers and basically everyone kept telling me it was time to get serious about school, but for me, getting serious meant getting stressed out. Instead of loving school, I started dreading it. Then I started procrastinating. Then I started having panic attacks. No bueno.

Tay, age 16: Up 'til around age eleven, I spent a lot of time with kids from my neighborhood playing outside, making up games, being feral. We never ran out of things to do. Around eleven or maybe twelve, I thought I was too cool. I started playing video games with my brother.

Jules, age 17: I used to like playing sports, but when I got to high school, it stopped being fun. I had no free time, and something I loved turned into something I hated. Winning became everything, and if you have an off day, you feel like it's the end of the world. When I tried to quit, everyone warned me that I shouldn't because sports look good on college apps—like you're supposed to sell your soul for college.

Gia, age 18: I used to take a lot of dance. I loved it when I was little, but I took a break when school got harder and more demanding. I'm afraid to go back because I'll be behind the girls who never left. (Interviewer: Can you go back just because you like it?) I wish. No, I'd suck and feel stupid.

Notice how each girl became separated from her natural passion once too much pressure or judgment entered the picture. Girls get so many different kinds of pressure—to grow up, to be amazing, to look amazing, to hide fear and vulnerability. No wonder many bail on the very sources of joy that used to light them up.

As new standards and expectations pop up in every direction, what makes you strong and happy and authentically you often gets buried under a fat pile of busyness, pressure, and striving. Falling short in any area means fear of disappointing people—or being judged, scolded, rejected, even bullied.

BALANCE

It's good to challenge yourself by working hard, and to hang in there even (and especially) when things get difficult. You just need to prioritize balance. A balanced life makes time for laughter, creativity, rest, and play. A balanced life protects you from swerving off your path into the miserable ditch of overwhelm and anxiety.

To achieve balance means you must *counterbalance* work and stress with rest and play. Not only do rest and play delight your soul, they're restorative.

Balance is the key to your physical health, your emotional health, your mental health—you get the picture. It's important! Would you run a 10K and then go to the gym? Of course not. Your body would collapse. Well, same with the rest of you. Your mind, your body, *and* your soul all need replenishing. Sleep, good food, and hydration are essential. But so is something else …!

PLAYDATES

You don't need to dig out your face paint to resurrect play in your life. You're probably drawn to different ways of playing these days. Being silly with your friends, laughing with your family, ambushing someone (whom you can outrun) with a water balloon, filling a baby pool and starfishing in it on a hot day, wrapping yourself in a blanket like a human burrito on a cold one—all fabulous examples of tapping into playfulness.

In a culture that won't stop pushing girls to grow up, dressing your dog up in doll clothes is the perfect antidote. Or making Mickey Mouse pancakes—because you freakin' feel like it. Or wearing sparkles some-where—because it's going to be a lo-o-o-o-ong day.

Play is not just for kids, which is why you sometimes see adults enjoy-ing Halloween *almost* a little too much. They're starved for play, too, and honestly, they need it. Here are a few more easy squeezy ideas for play: blowing bubbles, coloring, baking, baths, jumping rope, board games, crafts, art projects, napping outdoors, romping in nature, walking bare-foot, running through sprinklers, crazy hairdos, sparkles, random acts of dancing and singing.

The idea is to let your soul choose what you want to do. The part of you that's striving needs a break and your soul wants to play … possibly in a tree. See how it works? One idea leads to another, and pretty soon, your soulful essence is waking up and telling you what it wants and needs.

Every soul is endlessly nuanced and unique, so listen to yours and make time to follow its desires. When you practice listening to the whis-pers of your soul, it will start speaking more loudly and clearly and you'll feel more like your soulful self again.

Noodle This: How have you played lately? What play did you love as a child? Can you think of any ways you could put more play in your life?

> Ruby, 15: I got a onesie for my birthday with unicorns on it and yep, I wear it around the house. When I have a bad day, I come home and rock my onesie. It helps me take myself less seriously and it makes me happy.

HAPPINESS AS A BY-PRODUCT

Speaking of happiness, ever heard anyone say: "All I want is for you to be happy"? While well meant, that's a tricky thing to hear. It makes a lot of girls begin a habit of "happiness checking"—checking themselves to see if they're happy. Since happiness, like all feelings, comes and goes, you may feel like you're failing or that something is wrong with you because you're not happy.

The good news is: Nope, nothing's necessarily wrong. No one is happy all the time, and instead of shooting for a continuous feeling of happiness, you're better off shooting for things you can control more directly: self-care, soul care, putting your heart into the things you care about. These are things you can control, and guess what? When you pay attention to these things, you get more moments of happiness!

Happiness is a by-product of prioritizing the good things and the important things in life. It's like a party favor for showing up at the right party. Embrace it when it comes, and don't judge yourself when it goes. Just keep your eye on living a balanced life with plenty of soul care, and happiness will be a regular visitor.

DAILY BOWL OF SOUL

So here's the plan: you're going to do some tiny tweaks that support your reclamation of soulfulness. Since soul care is deeply personal, no two girls will be called to the same practices in the same way. As you absorb the ideas ahead, get a sense of what will work for you, and of course, give yourself full rein to explore, expand, reject, or tweak any of the examples so they reflect your unique soulfulness.

The timing for this tip is perfect since (remember!) you're trimming tech, which will feel weird and unnatural. Why not fill that space with a little soulfulness? After all, it was there first. Soul-care is part of self-care and without exception, girls who reclaim it feel better and better. Let's go!

SIX TIPS FOR SOUL RECLAMATION

Start by taking a sec to fix yourself a soothing cup of tea or whatever makes you happy. Then snuggle in for some pleasure reading because reclaiming soulfulness is a pleasure.

As you make your tea, slow yourself down and resist productive effi-ciency. Soulfulness isn't just what you do but how you do it. Let your soul choose your mug, and trust what it decides in the first three seconds before thinking comes in. Same with choosing your tea. Explore letting your soul lead this little ritual by vibing more from your heart than your head.

Not a tea drinker? Try this ritual with a simple glass of water, and if you have some citrus around, squeeze a bit in. Small gestures of soulful-ness are about the process as well as the outcome, so enjoy the whole shebang from prep to slurp.

Soul Tip 1: Create a Regular Soul-Affirming Ritual

You just completed a simple but powerful ritual. It slowed down your nervous system and gave balance to your mind-body connection. The more you put into that ritual, by really getting into your five senses, the more balance you gained.

Rituals are behaviors you set up and follow regularly. There are endless possibilities, and the one you did above, preparing a mindful cup of tea, is a great start. Here's another great one: gratitude practice.

Every morning, wake up and instead of going on your phone, name three things you're grateful for. It's a double win because starting your day by getting sucked into social media checking stokes anxiety while gratitude practice stokes feelings of well-being. Just lie in bed and think of your three things. They can be very small and simple; for example, *I'm grateful for the waffle I'm going to make myself in a few minutes. I'm grateful for the softness of my kitty. I'm grateful that I feel more or less ready for my math quiz today.*

The more you embrace your gratitude practice, the better. It's kind of like dialing your attitude to a positive setting before starting your day. You'll go on to absorb the good things more easily because you've primed your perceptual system to register and appreciate the good things in life.

During your day, note more things that you're grateful for and become amazing at absorbing positive vibes. Gratitude is vitamin G for the soul. People who count their blessings with a gratitude practice report feeling happier, exercising more, enjoying fewer physical complaints, and even sleeping better than those who create lists of hassles. It's an easy practice that increases a sense of soulful appreciation and connection to joy. Who doesn't want a slice of that?

Nerd Alert: Author, researcher, and speaker Brené Brown, notes a powerful relationship between joy and gratitude. Focusing on gratitude starts your day off on the right foot. According to Brown: "It's not joy that makes us grateful, but gratitude that makes us joyful." Check out Brené Brown's TED Talks. Life changing! She also has other presentations and interviews you can find online.

Special Note: As you know, not all screen time has the same impact on your well-being. Using screen time for self-improvement, self-education, and inspiration is positive and leads to feeling better. Screens are amazing for certain things—like watching TED Talks!

Soul Tip 2: Practice Everyday Mindfulness

If you hear the word "meditation" and cringe at the prospect of sitting motionless in lotus position while chanting a mantra or—even more challenging—clearing your mind of all thoughts, relax your cringe. You don't have to do that!

Mindfulness meditation is something your soulful self already knows how to do, and you don't even need to keep still while you do it. Author and meditation researcher Jon Kabat-Zinn defines it as "paying attention in a particular way, on purpose, in the present moment, nonjudgmentally."

If you were that little girl who ate sprinkles off your cupcake with great care, you were in a mindful state. As you used your tiny fingers to pluck the blue sprinkle, then the yellow sprinkle, then the green sprinkle, you were unconcerned with overthinking the process. You simply followed your soul's natural enjoyment.

Well, time to reclaim that beautiful mindfulness by connecting it to an everyday activity. Eating is a great time to be mindful, and if cupcakes aren't on the menu, any food will do. Try this:

For one meal or snack a day, practice mindfulness by paying attention fully to each bite you take. Notice all the information available to your five senses: the way that bite looks, smells, and feels in your mouth. The feel of your fork in your hand and the sound of it touching the plate. Fully notice the taste and texture of each bite.

To take this mindfulness one step further, put your fork down as each bite of food enters your mouth and just chew. When you've fully chewed each bite, pick up your fork again for the next. Take your time, breathe, and be present.

People notice several things when they eat mindfully. They enjoy their food more, eat more slowly, digest better, and get full faster. When life is busy, it's easy to inhale your food without really enjoying it. Treat yourself to full satisfaction and all the benefits of mindful eating by practicing it once a day.

You might feel a little weird or self-conscious doing this practice in certain settings, so feel free to modify it in order to be more low profile. Another option is practicing mindful eating during a solo snack or with someone who supports what you're doing. It may be hard to do this exercise without experiencing a thousand urges to grab your phone, but be strong and stick with it. You're cultivating your anxiety-free self plus: You can do hard things!

Other everyday mindfulness possibilities:

- Take a mindful bath or shower.

- Do an everyday chore mindfully—like making your bed.

- Take a mindful walk.

The keys to making your activities mindful are slowing way down and focusing on your five senses. It's natural to get distracted by thoughts, so just notice your distraction, label it "thinking," and gently redirect yourself back to the experience of your senses. In the shower, for example, you'd go back to noticing the feeling of the water, the smell of the soap, and so on.

Nerd Alert: Next time you crave tech time, use it to search "mindfulness" and learn more. Or search for "Jon Kabat-Zinn, MD" on YouTube. He's the guy who brought mindfulness into the mainstream, and you can hear him talk about, and even lead you in, guided meditation. He's very soothing and has a great voice.

Soul Tip 3: Take a Nature Bath

Has it been a while since you felt the simple pleasure of grass beneath your feet? According to a study sponsored by the Environmental Protection Agency, the average American spends 93 percent of their time indoors. Ouch! What a soul harsher.

What better way to soothe the stresses of the day than a nature bath? In Japan, there is a practice called *shinrin-yoku*, which means "forest bathing." The idea behind shinrin-yoku is to drink up natural surroundings through the five senses. Even small amounts of forest bathing are believed to have profoundly positive effects on you. Not only are you typically tech-free in nature, you're absorbing the sights, sounds, and vibes of the natural world.

Leah, age 20: Nature is actually the best way to soothe my anxiety. It gives me perspective, and it gets me out of my head. We have some great trails close to my campus that

I hike with whoever's around. You can also have great conversations with people when you're hiking. Something about nature just opens people up. By the time I'm back, I feel a shift that takes me through the rest of my day.

Walking in nature also involves moving your body, breathing clean air, and ramping down your nervous system, which is likely chronically overstimulated. A raft of research indicates that time in nature has positive effects on mood and aspects of cognitive function, including working memory. Best of all, it has a quieting effect on anxiety.

Noodle This: Is there a way you can get more nature bathing into your life? Many teens are not thrilled with being asked by their parents to go on hikes or walks or bike rides, but when they do, they're glad they did. Noodle ideas with parents or friends that could open doors to being outside more often.

Special Note: Some teen girls feel understimulated, not overstimulated. They have too much free time and struggle with loneliness and way too much screen time. There are lots of reasons girls can be underengaged, and if this is you, be gentle with yourself, but also firm. Too much indoor time can put you in a bubble that traps you into a limited perspective of your capabilities. Is there a way you can get yourself out in the open air more often? Identify caring people in your life who can support you in getting out more often.

Soul Tip 4: Make Scents for Your Soul

Have you ever caught a whiff of something—let's say cookies baking—and felt a cascade of positive emotions?

Nerd Alert: The smell center in your brain (aka your olfactory bulb) is part of your *limbic system*, the region of the brain in charge of emotional processing. That's why good smells can equal powerful, pleasant emotions and memories. With this fabulous factoid in mind, let's make sure you use this info to your emotional advantage.

Aromatherapy makes use of the connection between emotions and scents, and getting started can be easy. According to holistic health coach Jessica Betancourt:

> If you're experiencing moments of depression or anxiety, essential oils can offer fantastic relief. Geranium, vetiver, and frankincense all have a calming, grounding effect, and citrus oils like lemon, grapefruit, and orange can lift the spirit! Place several drops of the oil(s) of your choice into the palms of your hands, and briskly rub together to warm and activate the essential oil's properties. Place your cupped hands over your nose, close your eyes, and take three to five deep inhalations.
>
> Now add a bit of a carrier oil (a neutral oil like olive, jojoba, coconut, or almond to dilute the essential oil and protect the skin from possible sensitivities, or a fragrance-free lotion) to your palms, and massage this blend into the back of your neck and over your heart chakra.

While aromatherapy isn't a cure for anxiety, research is showing that it's proving gangbusters at reducing many of its symptoms. Unlike prescription medications and other traditional means of treatment, aromatherapy is both safe and cost-effective.

Kelsey, age 19: I keep a small tin of rose-scented lip balm in my backpack at all times. I like that I can very low key apply a little to my lips and at the same time, get a whiff of rose. I'm in cosmetology school and it's very demanding, so I appreciate all the help I can get.

Soul Tip 5: Create Random Acts of Beauty

The purest way to create art is for the enjoyment of it. Little girls know that, which is why they love art. They adore massaging paintbrushes into paint colors and don't care that purple polka-dotted trees don't actually exist in nature. Before little girls start judging their talents and skills, they do a lot of things for the joy of it. Reclaiming soulfulness means reaching back into that spirit of doing and being, just because it feels good.

Reality: Sometimes growing up is a buzzkill. When your inner critic kicks in, fun can really go out the window. Singing, dancing, making music, listening to music, making art, looking at art—all things the soul loves!

Julia, age 19: I'm busy in college but as often as I can, I layer self-care by hitting multiple targets at the same time: (1) I exercise in nature and (2) create random acts of beauty (3) on my walks and hikes. My favorite thing is to make rock sculptures, which basically means I stack rocks on top of each other and perch them in whimsical places. I made a heart out of twigs once. Sometimes I just draw things in the dirt with sticks. I like the idea of other hikers coming upon my little creations.

There are so many ways to express soulfulness creatively when you get out of the box and into your true nature. Some girls enjoy being creative with their appearance—hair, makeup, clothes. Sparkles tend to make the soul smile. Some girls like to decorate their bicycles or backpacks with flowers or whatever. You can even combine a random act of kindness with a random act of beauty. Why not put a flower in your ponytail holder *and* give one to someone who looks like they could use it?

Soul Tip 6: Look Up and Connect

Another quick dip in a bath full of soulfulness: Next time you're in the car or waiting in line and passing time looking down at your phone, look up and connect with the people around you. Before phones, people did this all the time and benefited from it.

Researchers have found that chatting in line, making small talk with the people around you, greeting people as you walk by and exchanging pleasantries unleashes a cascade of brain chemicals that enhance your sense of well-being and human connection. What another great reason to ghost your phone.

Noodle This: Do something every day without having your phone on you. As in: *at all.* As in: *actually leaving it at home or in the car.* This will feel as natural as leaving your hand at home—not natural at all. But you can do it. Your soul craves it!

As you do that something, be fully present in your environment. Connect with people and your surroundings. As long as you're in a safe setting, practice greeting your fellow humans with a little friendly eye contact or a smile. If you end up in a line somewhere, engage in a bit of mindless chatting. It will not only give your brain chemicals a nice boost, it will make you feel more connected and less insulated in your own bubble.

More connection is an antianxiety boost. In fact, since human connection and healthy relationships are a huge part of your mental health and happiness, the next tip focuses on strengthening your ability to have the best relationships possible. No need to leave soulfulness behind though. It's something you can take with you wherever you go. Time for Tip 8!

Navigate Social Stress

*For beautiful eyes, look for the good in others; for
beautiful lips, speak words of kindness.*

—Audrey Hepburn

Some of the best moments of your day involve your friends. There's nothing like a well-chosen GIF, a hilarious text, or the sight of a friend's face to add a puff of comfort and connection to your life. Not only are friends people you can have fun with, close friends are people you can confide in. Despite how teen girls are portrayed in movies and shows, the truth is that most are very devoted and loving in friendships. In general, your social life adds a sense of connection and stability to your life.

Except when it doesn't.

Okay, so life can get complicated. Sometimes out of nowhere, things in a friendship go sideways. Someone feels hurt, betrayed, insecure, abandoned, annoyed—and sometimes that person is you.

Problems in your social life are often a big trigger for anxiety. It makes sense: relationships offer security—conflict feels like a threat to security—your brain's smoke alarm activates in the face of threat—*boom!* Anxiety.

No matter how sensible and considerate you and your friends *usually* are, everyone has blind spots, weak moments, bad moods, tender feelings, and room to grow in social skillfulness.

> Lena, age 14: I hate conflict. When I'm upset with a friend, I try to ignore it until it goes away. Or I avoid the friend for a while.

> Mila, age 16: I don't like confrontation. I freeze up and panic, both at the same time. Weird but possible.

> Annabelle, age 15: I have one friend that I can bring things up with, and it's actually made us closer because we both really listen. Mainly I think girls get so defensive that there's really no point in bringing things up. Everyone knows there's tension, but no one really addresses it directly.

Both Lena and Mila equate conflict with crisis, which drives up their anxiety and avoidance behaviors. The way you perceive things has a *lot* to do with how you experience them.

Annabelle, in contrast, seems to have a different attitude toward conflict. In her friendship, there's a sense of safety in sharing feelings. Both Annabelle and her friend place a high value on listening to one another with openness, which makes it easier for each of them to bring up tensions that arise.

NORMALIZING CONFLICT

Hopefully, you're learning to normalize a lot of the anxiety that comes and goes throughout your day. The less you panic in response to anxiety, the weaker it gets and the less it shows up in all its usual places.

Nerd Alert: To *normalize* something means to realize and accept it as normal, not pathological or a sign that something is terribly wrong.

Same thing with conflict! If you normalize it, see it as natural and inevitable, you'll be stronger in the face of it—and able to handle it better. In the real world, conflict among friends is normal. Until the day comes when people mutate into cyborgs, who share one mind and personality, people will have differences, and differences—occasionally— bring conflict.

A good mind-set about conflict is to accept that occasional social flare-ups are part of life—not a sign of doom or disaster. Conflicts only degrade into disaster when handled very badly.

If you perceive an issue in your social life as a crisis, you may either (1) freeze and stuff your feelings, or (2) act on impulse, meaning react on emotion, without consideration of the impact.

WHICH ONE ARE YOU?

Think about a recent or memorable social conflict you've had. When things go sideways, do you have an automatic way of responding?

Are You a Freezer?

Freezers equate social tension and conflict with danger and crisis. Freezers describe literally experiencing a "freeze" feeling emotionally and physically. Anxiety hits Freezers hard.

Freezing is an understandable response to conflict. In a stressful social moment, your brain may prompt you to freeze in order to minimize risk or danger. If you remain in a social freeze state, it probably means you are stuffing a lot of feelings down in order to maintain your freeze mode.

Here's the problem with that: Remember the naked savages from Tip 4? Aka your feelings?

Well, they don't like to be trapped or crowded. If you do either, your wild guys will pretty much torture you from within. (Feelings are claustrophobic and need movement.) You may get stuck obsessing about the situation and even suffer physical symptoms such as exhaustion, stomachaches, or headaches. Stuffing feelings comes at a cost.

Are You a Reactor?

Reactors express their upset, often quickly and with great emotion. Reactors often experience less anxiety right away because they're venting it out all around them. In the bigger picture, anxiety often catches up with a Reactor because the venting (aka gossiping) creates additional conflict.

Acting on impulse means the wild guys pop out of you like caffeinated ninjas with access to microphones. They end up creating more problems because impulsive actions are often emotionally driven and not deeply considered. Emotional discharges may feel good in the moment, only to make things worse in the bigger picture.

Here's an example: One of your friends has been in a bad mood lately, and you seem to be her target. The jabs add up, and in a flare-up of hurt and anger, you unleash your frustration about her onto several of your other friends. If this doesn't describe you, maybe you've been in one of the other two positions: the friend being talked about *or* a friend who witnesses the vent sesh. No position in this scenario is fun. It sucks to feel upset with a friend, it sucks to be the person who is talked about, and it sucks to feel yourself in the middle of a friend's conflict.

The truth about gossip? While reacting impulsively via venting is 100 percent understandable (you're hurt/angry and in need of support), coming in hot to friends about another friend often stimulates full-blown drama. Most girls have experienced being on different sides of gossip and know it has a way of both leaking *and* making listeners uncomfortable.

Or a kind of negative bonding occurs through processing the gossip. Negative because of the judgment and criticism (even though it may seem justified) and because each person involved becomes quietly aware that they, too, could be the focus of such gossip someday; that is, *If we're talking about X like this, I could be talked about in just the same way.*

When you're in the position of needing to vent, take a moment to care for your feelings. Venting in your journal can help you express and clarify your feelings. Venting about a friend to a family member or person outside your social circle is often a better choice than involving friends inside the group. You get relief and support, plus you protect yourself, your friend, and the group from a tidal wave of social tension.

The bottom line: In conflict situations, girls gossip not because they're "backstabbing bitches," but because they're feeling extremely upset—often vulnerable—and desperate for validation and support.

While nothing will remove all social conflict from your life, knowing how to manage it helps you also manage anxiety. There's a truism that you can't control what happens in life, only how you respond to it. Accepting conflict as normal and inevitable, and knowing how to handle it, helps you be strong and confident in all your relationships.

Are You a Navigator?

To grow beyond freezing or reacting, it helps to learn and practice a third option: being a Navigator. Navigators may start off freezing *or* wanting to vent—but they resist getting trapped in either reaction. Instead, Navigators notice their emotions and navigate thoughtfully.

Madi, age 15: I've learned the hard way to be a Navigator. I used to freeze and withdraw when anything came up that was hard or stressful. I had no confidence in myself to handle it right. I had tons of anxiety all through middle school for this reason, plus I was kind of a doormat. I think when you don't respect yourself, other people don't respect you either. I still feel the impulse to freeze, but now I know that means I need to make time to sort through my feelings and decide what I want to do.

A good rule of thumb in conflict is to *first take care of yourself.* You've been building a loving, caring relationship with yourself tip by tip—and all that work comes with a payoff! As you become more solid with you, handling all the challenges in your life comes more easily.

Navigators first take time to sit with their emotions in order to better understand them, while also giving the emotions time to settle. Whatever you decide to do, things always go better when you're coming from an emotionally calm and coherent state.

Next you can decide if you want to communicate about the conflict with the person or people involved. While well-meaning support people often urge others to "just tell her how you feel," that's a decision for you to make thoughtfully.

For example, if your feelings are strongly affected by whatever happened (or is happening), you may want to speak up. If you're only mildly upset, you may choose to let it go. If you do let it go, but the issue resurfaces, you can always change your mind and decide to address it after all.

Another consideration: How important is the person you have the conflict with? If the person isn't very important to you, you may want to let the issue pass. If the person is important, it makes sense to address it through skillful communication.

COMMUNICATION DOS

Okay, so let's say you're working on being a Navigator. You've taken time to care for your feelings and evaluate whether or not your social conflict warrants communication. You're feeling more settled, but still upset about the situation that's causing you social distress. The person you have a conflict with is important to you. You're ready to communicate. These dos will help things go well.

Do: Give a Heads-Up

Often one person feels social conflict, while the other person involved is oblivious. We all have blind spots that make it hard to see and experience ourselves the way other people do. No matter what a sweetie pie you are down deep, you have the capacity to hurt someone and not even know it. Assume the person you're upset with also has blind spots and may be oblivious about the hurt she caused you. Try: *Hey, can we talk for a minute after practice? I want to touch base with you about something.* Or even text: *Can I call you later? I want to talk something through with you.*

Ideally, you follow up with a face-to-face talk. Important convos go much better when you can make eye contact and imbue your communication with consideration to tone and body language. Even when you're angry—especially when you're angry—it helps to convey goodwill to whomever you're speaking to.

Nerd Alert: "Goodwill" means friendly, helpful, or cooperative feelings or attitude. Having goodwill toward the person you're talking to is easier when you come from a belief that few people in life *intend* to harm you. Most conflicts are due to unconscientious behavior—not evil intention. Since all of us are vulnerable to getting stuck in our own bubble (me, me, me), we're all capable of unintentionally hurting people we care about.

Exception: Some friendships are just plain toxic. If you have a friend who repeatedly criticizes you, lies to you, flakes on you, and fails to show signs of genuine care for you, moving on may be the healthiest choice.

Do: Start Right

A *harsh start-up* is a term in psychology that describes a hostile approach to communication; for example, *I heard what you said about me not coming to Meghan's birthday barbecue, and I think it was really a bitch move on your part.*

The worst part about a harsh start-up is that it shuts down the listener, who fails to see your pain and sees only your hostility. Also, you're robbing your listener of the benefit of the doubt by assuming what you heard is absolutely true and accurate. Instead, try: *I want to check something out with you. I heard you called me a flake for not coming to Meghan's barbecue. I heard you think I blow off my friends to be with my boyfriend, but before assuming that's completely accurate, I wanted to talk to you about it.*

Do: Lay on the Goodwill

Since you've made the decision to communicate, there's a good chance that whoever you're talking to means something to you. It's excruciatingly hard for teen girls to be solid and accountable in a conflict. The reason is that it's hard to hear that you've blown it and hurt someone.

In general, teen girls are extremely aware of and caring about the feelings of other people. That being said, and as noted above, everyone has blind spots, weak moments, bad moods, tender feelings, and room to grow in social skillfulness. Everyone!

Here are examples of how you might infuse your communication with goodwill:

- *I'm bringing this up because I consider you a good friend and a good person.*

- *I know we can work through this. I just need to address something I'm noticing because I don't want it to negatively affect our friendship.*

- *I'm talking to you directly because I respect you as a person and a friend and I don't want to keep this inside to fester.*

When you infuse your communication with plenty of goodwill, you help your friend hear your feedback in the context of the bigger—more positive and comforting—picture.

Noodle This: If you were to receive feedback from a friend who is upset with something you've said or done, what kind of goodwill would be comforting to you?

Olivia, age 18: I just had this happen and my friend said, "You know I love the hell out of you—but—you're making me late to school and if you don't get better at being ready when I pick you up, I'm going to leave without you." Her point was super clear—and I deserved it—but she's so good at making me feel secure in our friendship that I don't lose it when she calls me out. I just try to be better!

Now that you've got some dos under your belt, here's some advice from a grad student who considers herself an excellent social Navigator.

Taylor, age 24: I come from a very communicative family. My mother gives seminars on how to communicate in the workplace, and my father is a therapist who works with high-conflict families and couples. They taught me that speaking directly to people is the best way to address conflict, and they also taught me not to fear conflict because when you handle it well, it actually makes relationships stronger. Think about it: Don't you trust the friend who has the courage to speak to you about problems? Don't you feel like you have value to that person? Otherwise, they wouldn't bother!

Taylor boils her approach down to three steps:

1. Describe the problem.

Without blaming or bringing in confrontational energy, I'll ask a friend if we can make time to talk. In person is always best because there's more humanity in the interaction, and you can create the tone you want with your voice and attitude. Then I keep it very simple and just describe the problem; for example, "It feels like you've been canceling on me a lot lately," or "I've noticed you've been too busy to hang out lately."

2. Share your feelings.

I keep this short and sweet because laying it on really thick gives the other person too much responsibility and often causes a shutdown or a defensive response. So I'll say something like: "I'm bummed because I miss you." Often, the other person takes the convo at this point and since I'm good at conveying good vibes instead of critical vibes, I often get a good response. Other times, I go on to the next step.

3. Ask for what you need.

Again, I keep this simple. In the example of missing a friend, maybe I'd ask if we could try for a regular coffee date or something. Right now, I'm in grad school and have a situation I just dealt with recently. I had a group project with a classmate who kept flaking on his part, so with him I said: (1) "It's been a pattern that you're late with your part of the project," (2) "That's frustrating for me because I'm doing my part and I want to do well in this class," and (3) "I'm hoping you can do whatever you need to do to be more accountable to our group and our project deadlines." He took it pretty well. People want to give excuses so I listened to his but didn't soften my point. Hopefully, he'll show he's accountable by leveling up.

Do: Be Accountable

Being accountable in your friendships means you say what you mean and you mean what you say. In general, you follow through with plans and are someone your friends can trust and count on. Flakiness is annoying, and people tend to perceive it as a lack of respect or a sign that they're not being valued.

In conflicts, being accountable means you listen to a friend who brings up an issue with you and you open your mind and heart to feedback. In Taylor's example, her classmate grumbled out some excuses but heard what she said and hopefully will make the change she asked for.

When being accountable to a friend, you'll find it's easier when that friend approaches you skillfully, as in the examples above.

Unfortunately, most girls will not know how to bring things up in a calm and skillful way. Lots of people hate conflict so much that they stuff their feelings and stuff their feelings until they explode. When that happens, there's more heat and raw emotion than skill—and that's hard for anyone to handle.

When you're the recipient of an explosion, it can be very hard to listen with an open mind and heart. Instead, instinct is often to counter-attack or get defensive.

Do: Avoid Defensiveness

This is a tough one, especially when someone is coming in hot or is completely off base with what they're mad about (or both—ugh!). It helps to remember that the feeling that drives anger is often hurt. The angriest people in the world are the most hurt.

Sometimes it helps to say, *I want to hear what you have to say, but I think talking will be more productive when we're both calm.*

Upon hearing the words *I want to hear what you have to say*, the angry person will often take it down a notch. If not, stand your ground and repeat what you need in order to have a productive conversation. It's easier to hear someone when they're not breathing fire at you.

Dana, age 21: I live with four other women, and we've had our share of conflicts. I used to be super defensive because I was so panicked about being confronted. I think the most defensive people are the ones that have the hardest time accepting that it's okay to make a mistake. Think about it— if you're okay not being perfect, you're just going to listen and apologize. If you think you have no room for error in relationships, you're going to be defensive. And that will make everything worse because upset people just want to be acknowledged. Now I accept that I'm not here to be perfect, I'm gonna annoy my housemates from time to time, and it's not the end of the world. I can just hear them out, apologize, and learn from it. We are all close, so I know conflict doesn't hurt relationships when it's handled well.

Do: Make a Good Repair

Research reveals that conflict doesn't hurt relationships as long as it's followed by attempts to repair the rupture. Navigators are good at apology and repair because they've learned through experience that repair is magic balm on emotional burns.

Navigators are good at keeping an eye on the true prize: creating the desired outcome. If your desired outcome is to be right and make another person wrong, the repair process will go poorly. If your desired outcome is to listen and be heard then apologize when necessary, accept an apology when offered; your outcome will be a stronger, closer relationship.

These magic words can help with a good repair:

- *I hear what you're saying and I can see why that upset you.*

- *I care about your feelings/our friendship and I'd never want to hurt you.*

- *I'm glad you're sharing your feelings.*

- *I'll work on what you've brought to my attention and try to do better.*

- *Is there anything else you'd like to hear from me to help make this better?*

Learning to be accountable instead of defensive is life-changing in relationships. Tap into a loving and generous place and try it next time you have the opportunity.

Do: Allow for Social Fluidity

In both your freshman year of high school and your freshman year of college, you may start with a couple of friends or a friend group that you eventually migrate away from. This can happen at any time, but it's especially common at these junctures.

Migrations happen because starting new, in each situation, often prompts bonding with whomever you already know—or meet first. In high school, you often hang close to the kids you know from middle school. In college, you often bond with the friends you meet first in your dorm or orientation or classes. In an eagerness to feel the security of connection, you often bond with the connections that are most readily available.

In time, however, you may notice the ways in which your original homies are not the best fit for you. Be open to the idea that it's natural to gravitate away from some people in order to move closer to others. It's actually very common and natural.

> Catherine, age 22: I have migrated out of friend groups a few times in my life. In high school, I found I felt more comfortable with my athlete friends than my middle school friends. There wasn't a dramatic breakup, just an incremental shift that worked out okay for everyone. Same in college. My best friends now that I'm a senior are not the friends I started off with as a freshman. My best advice is that it's better to make changes than to be in a group that isn't a good fit for you.

Catherine adds that, most of the time, migrating friend groups is low drama: As long as you behave decently to everyone, most people will accept natural fluctuations in friend groups. In one case, I had a friend come to me and let me know she missed me. At that point, I felt more open to her and so we reconnected, but I didn't go back to that larger friend group. I just didn't feel on the same page with them.

Rather than being the one who is migrating, you may have a friend who drifts away from you or your friend group. If the loss feels significant, you can talk with that friend about it. If you perceive the migration as normal and natural, you can touch base with her in a way that is more curious and less accusingly confrontational.

Do: Go for Quality Over Quantity

It's easy to assume that having a big group of friends is an ideal scenario. But is it really?

Sara, age 14: I've always really liked the idea of having a big group of friends. It feels like those kids at my school are having the most fun.

In truth, girls in big groups are not necessarily more socially satisfied than girls with one to three solid friends. In fact, bigger groups come with bigger challenges:

- how to handle not liking one of the group members

- how to handle inviting one or two people, but not the entire group, without hurting feelings

- how to support one friend who is mad at another in the group, especially when you don't have a problem with that person

If you have one to three good friends that you trust and have fun with, you possibly have an ideal scenario. Not only do you really like and count on those friends, you don't have to navigate as many side issues. Bigger groups often deal with more drama, more tension, more insecurity, and more anxiety about who is closer to whom.

On top of all that, because it's not natural to like all people equally, teens in bigger groups often stuff down—or talk about—group members they struggle with. When it comes to big groups, size and visibility don't equal more fun or happiness.

Now that you have a handle on conflict, you'll be in a much better position to navigate through the natural social tensions that present themselves in your relationships. It takes time to resculpt an "OMG" response into an "I've got this" response, so be patient, yet committed, to practicing new habits.

Let's move on to Tip 9 where we address another common source of anxiety for teen girls: academics.

Be a Healthy Achiever

In order to kick ass, you must first lift your foot.

—Jen Sincero

You know how it sometimes feels like adults don't really get the pressure you're under? Well, you've got a point. It's not that they don't want to. It's just that so much has changed in the lives of teen girls that even the most well-meaning adults often struggle to fully grasp the pressures you face.

Most adults simply lived much different lives when they were teens:

- They went to school (which was much less demanding and stressful).

- They had an activity (which required minimal time, energy, and commitment).

- They chilled out with friends (there was *way more* chilling with friends—in person).

- They had part-time jobs (which stoked feelings of independence and personal empowerment).

- They did homework (not excruciating amounts).

- They went to bed (scant technology made eight to ten hours easy).

Pretty easy breezy.

There was plenty of time to contemplate the meaning of life, get to know themselves, explore fun, be adventurous and independent, even do nothing but just plain be. To make things even more teen friendly, college wasn't typically a talking point until around junior year of high school.

FROM BREEZY TO QUEASY

As you've suspected, things are more intense for your generation. Are there more opportunities for girls than ever before? Yes! There are significantly more offerings in every direction: classes, sports, clubs, volunteer opportunities, and activities. And guess what? Girls are absolutely *slaying* in all those areas. That's the upside.

The downside is that there are many more places, areas, and ways for girls to expect a lot of themselves. High expectations call for the allocation of time, effort, energy, and commitment—not a bad thing *if* you're realistic about the limits of your human capabilities.

Unrealistic expectations set girls up for anxious concern about how to make everything work and how to get everything done. Depending on what your commitments are and who is in charge, requirements can be so taxing that what starts out with passion withers in burnout.

More than boys, girls place high value on doing just about everything extremely well, and they take it hard in a very personal way when they come up short. In your parents' teen years, girls may have had one or two commitments beyond school. Today's teen girl often expects herself to achieve everything: strong academics, amazing relationships, killer SAT scores, being liked, being admired, being respected, looking great, being fit, being stylish, being a good person, making people happy, making people proud … it's a lot.

And because girls are often wicked critics of themselves, they're vulnerable to getting stuck in chronic disappointment over perceived shortcomings.

When tons of busyness tangles together with superhigh expectations, you can always find anxiety lurking in a backpack nearby. It's a high-risk mind-set that positions girls to feel chronically wired, tired, and disappointed.

Tip 9 is here with great news about achievement: you can be a healthy high achiever who balances doing her best with maintaining reasonable balance and self-care. Let's get you started!

When you get control of achievement, you move from Whac-a-Mole mode to checkers mode. Instead of smacking things down as they pop up, you take a look at your true priorities and approach them efficiently and realistically.

FROM REACTIVE TO INTENTIONAL

When it comes to designing your life, you want to think more checkers or chess than Whac-a-Mole. Playing checkers or chess requires thoughtful focus, observation, strategy, and consideration of the impact each move will make. Whac-a-Mole involves using a mallet to hit toy moles, which appear at random, forcing them back into their holes. The moves in checkers and chess are thoughtful, strategic, and *intentional*, whereas those in Whac-a-Mole are purely *reactive*.

When you take on too much and expect to do it all perfectly, without pausing to see what realistically makes sense for you, you may find yourself attacking your to-dos like the moles in Whac-a-Mole or—even more problematically—shutting down/procrastinating.

If you have a lot of interests and energy, you may say yes to things because they intrigue you. Such exuberance can backfire if you realize later that you scheduled yourself into another commitment—and out of time you could have spent doing other things that you value.

Reality time: *You can't do everything and you definitely can't do everything extremely well.*

Even more liberating, your value and worthiness on the planet are completely independent of what you're doing and how you're doing it. You may feel better when you're excelling, especially if you're maintaining health and balance. But you're not awesome because you get great grades. Achievements are merely the ornaments on your intrinsic awesomeness.

That's a hard one for a lot of teen girls, so don't worry if you don't totally buy it right now. Hopefully, in time you'll be able to deeply accept it as truth.

Noodle This: Write down your schedule representing everything you do all seven days of the week. Include homework time, social time, and sleep, making sure that you schedule nine hours for sleeping. Looking at your schedule, do you see time for self-care, rest, and fun? If not, what can you shave down or eliminate to allow more time for healthy balance?

Include important adults to help you think realistically about your commitments. Creating a reasonable schedule sets you up for success on every level. You deserve to have quality of life, and to have it, you need time for balance.

BURNOUT CONTROL

If you've been stressed about achievement for too long, you may be at risk (or already in) a state of academic burnout. When girls reach this level of wear and tear, they often report feeling empty, numb, and angry. It's a painful place to be.

If you're not sure, read through this list of red flags and get a sense of what's true for you.

- You've become more critical of your work and can't seem to go easier on yourself.

- You absolutely dread going to school.

- You absolutely dread homework, as if it's physical torture.

- Your energy level feels so low you wonder if there's something wrong with your health.

- When you get great results on a test or project, the good feeling fades fast and then you just feel anxious about the next thing you have to do.

- Focusing is hard. You find yourself googling ADD.

- You crave sugar and carbs, as if your body is looking for an energy source.

- You feel irritable with other people, especially those interrupting you or prompting you to get your work done.

- Your family members make salty comments about your attitude and how grumpy you are.

- You spend more time in meaningless distraction mode than you do in productivity mode. And if anyone comments, you want to scrape their face off.

- You're exhausted during the day but have trouble sleeping at night.

If you can relate to one or more of these bullet points, it's time to make some more changes to give you more oxygen in your life.

There's actually a safe and sane track to being your best while maintaining self-love, self-care, soul care, and overall balance. It's a good time to find it because when you do, you'll move toward your goals in a healthy, balanced way, without getting lost or too demoralized to continue. This stage of your life is an ideal time to make modifications, aka more baby steps for you!

ACHIEVEMENT STYLES

You can think of achievement styles as falling into one of three categories. You may have a perfectionistic style, which means you focus lots of energy into doing your absolute best—no matter what the cost. You may be a frustrated achiever, which means you'd like to do well, but feel chronically disappointed in your performance. Or you may be a healthy high achiever, which means you like to do your best, but within reason; you don't expect to be a rock star in every subject, and your preparation process is strong and efficient, with room for self-care.

Do you have a sense of which one you are? The best one, of course, is the sweet spot—healthy high achievement.

Noodle This: Notice your feelings about this vignette:

Two girls prepare for a class speech. One is a healthy high achiever (HHA), the other a perfectionist (P). They are both well prepared. The HHA is nervous but also excited because she feels more or less ready and looks forward to the speech being behind her. The P is nervous, not too excited, exhausted from lack of sleep, and also ready to have this speech off her plate so she can focus on other things.

Both girls do a great job. On the way back to her seat, the HHA feels cascading feelings of relief, satisfaction, and pride. On the way back to her seat, the P feels stressed, frustrated, and obsessed with a small part of her speech she's convinced could have been better. The HHA is radiating her happiness and relief. The P is joyless.

Let's look more closely at each style.

Perfectionist

The fuel driving perfectionism is fear, and the strategy driving perfectionism is shame avoidance. Perfectionists believe that if they excel in every possible way, no one will criticize them, reject them, or judge them as "not good enough." As Brené Brown notes, "when perfection is driving us, shame is riding shotgun, and fear is that annoying backseat driver."

Noodle This: That's a big and possibly brand-new way of seeing things, so read the preceding paragraph again and check in with your heart to see if it resonates. If it does, have compassion for yourself because perfectionism is a painful place to be. As you create more balance in your life, you will grow beyond seeing your value as determined by external measures, because your true value can't be measured that way. You are a person, not a performance, not a grade. You are not a product to be rated and reviewed.

When a high, high bar isn't hit, perfectionists lack resilience because their prime objective is outcome, not process. Not self-care or balance. Even when they hit the desired outcome, there's a noteworthy absence of true joy because it's hard to enjoy the destination when the journey sucks your soul dry.

> Kirstin, age 21: I graduated from high school with a 4.4 grade point average. I worked my ass off, was sleep deprived, cranky, unhappy, and anxious. I'd wake up anxious and be anxious all day. I can't believe I lived like that for so long and thought it was normal. I just wanted to make sure I got into the college I wanted. Long story short, I didn't. It was just a very competitive year for applicants, and when I got the news, I tanked. I got extremely depressed and resentful, and even though I got into other good schools, I fell apart.

Kirstin's depression became so serious that she began having suicidal thoughts. Luckily, she told her mom about her thoughts and they worked together to get Kirstin connected to a counselor. Over time, Kirstin modified her mind-set and adjusted her expectations to be more reasonable and self-caring. Here's what she says about healing her perfectionism:

> I had to change my internal world of thoughts, priorities, expectations. It was hard but so worth it to change my relationship with myself, my worth, my approach to pursuing school, and really, all my interests because I can go HAM on anything I do—which is not the good quality I thought it was. I now see perfectionism as an illness, or at least a risk factor

for illness. I ended up at a college I totally recognize as where I'm supposed to be. I'm grateful I didn't get into my "dream college." I do well but more than that, I live a balanced life that I actually like. I dropped a class I was able to recognize was a bad fit for me. I've gotten some Bs. Guess what? It's fine! Success is a bigger picture than just grades.

Top Tips to Tame Perfectionism

These tips come from recovering women perfectionists of all ages. They can help you get on a healthier track.

Do things in life you're not good at. Sing even if you're tone-deaf. Dance even if you have two left feet. Do fun things terribly and for the joy of it.

Love yourself more. When you do, being perfect matters less. Care more about how you feel than how you look to others.

Get help. Reach out to supportive friends or a therapist when you're in a flare-up. Say something like "I'm taking myself way too seriously right now and my perfectionism is paralyzing me. Can you tell me something reassuring?"

Pleasure read. There's nothing to achieve or memorize. Get lost in a book just because it feels good. That's what people did before phones and Netflix!

Do your absolute best sometimes (not all the time). Determine what's important and what's not. Take shortcuts sometimes in order to have work/life balance. Get the most important things done as well as you can, schedule less-important things out far enough to make execution reasonable—and eat lunch! Never skip the simple and pleasurable moments of life to run yourself into the ground.

Take breaks. Do this especially if you're working on a big project. When you come back to what you're doing, you'll bring added perspective to it, and it will be better in the long run.

Be self-aware. Show up for the cues your body presents you with. If you have a headache, if you're hungry or irritable, take time to figure out what you need and show up for that.

See the bigger picture. When you have big ambitions, plenty will go wrong along the way. And you'll learn from what goes wrong and keep moving. If you allow the little things to take you down, you won't be able to maintain the motivation to keep moving forward in spite of the setbacks.

Be efficient. Make a work plan that makes sense. Schedule in breaks and meals and time for consultation with others. Working blindly longer and longer, allowing yourself to indulge a million distractions, sets you up for panic and rage.

Soothe Perfectionism

Be kind to yourself as you modify your perfectionistic ways. Read the following affirmations to see how they impact your thoughts and feelings. Practice saying them, thinking them, and believing them. In time, you'll replace your perfectionistic mind-set with a healthier one!

I'm not my grade. A grade is a reflection of how I performed on this test/ assignment. It is not a statement about my intelligence or capabilities.

I'm not here to be perfect. I'm here to learn and live life fully.

I focus on effort, not outcome.

I'm a person, not a project.

Effort is in my circle of power; outcome is outside that circle. I love a good outcome, but I focus on effort and process because that's where I have power.

Pen Power: Make up a few self-soothers of your own and write them down in a notebook or somewhere you can read them and remind yourself of your developing healthy mind-set.

Frustrated Achievers

Some girls struggle with frustration and hopelessness about their abilities in school. If you feel that you work much harder than the kids you know and still don't get the grades you want, you may feel like a frustrated achiever. It's important to explore the possible sources of your frustration because if you understand the underlying causes, you can make adjustments that make a helpful difference.

Some frustrated achievers are setting goals that are too high. You may feel like you need to be the student your sibling is, or that your parents expect you to be. The problem with trying to hit the bar set by other people is that it may not be the right bar for you. The only bar that matters is the one that encourages you to be *your* best, not anyone else's best.

Some girls aren't fans of academics altogether but have passions and talents that aren't a focus in school. If this is you, talk to your counselor and other supportive adults so you can get what you need from school without setting yourself up for chronic disappointment. If you love art and not math, or dance but not science, do your best in school but accept that it's outside those subjects that you commune with passionate learning.

If you feel you're working hard in school but your grades just don't reflect your capabilities, there could be something getting in the way. For example, if you feel easily distracted, have a hard time paying attention in class, or notice specific areas of struggle—like understanding what you read—you may have a learning difference that's getting in your way.

Madison, age 15: I did okay in middle school but I noticed even then that I worked more slowly than my friends, who seemed to whip through their homework. Freshman year of high school was bad because the workload ramped up and my classes had a lot of reading. I started feeling really bad about myself and instead of working harder, I got kind of a bad attitude about school. I spent a lot of time on social media and watching shows—anything to distract myself. I got into some trouble, I think because I felt so bad, and started hanging out with friends who didn't care about school. In a blowup with my parents, I talked about how hard school was for me, and they brought up the idea that maybe I had a learning difference. My school helped me get an evaluation, and we found out I have dyslexia. I was relieved! Now it feels like we have a plan that gives me support so I can do my best.

Learning differences are not uncommon, and approximately one in five Americans have either a learning or an attentional difficulty! If you have one, you're in good company. Tons of famous, successful people do too. Do a quick internet search, and you will find a long and impressive list of people who have figured out how to achieve great things anyway. In fact, many experts believe that having a learning difference gives people a unique way of looking at the world that helps create success.

Nerd Alert: Malcom Gladwell's *David and Goliath* is a great book or audiobook if you're interested in fascinating stories and research about the surprising gifts that come with such struggles.

If you suspect you might have a learning difference, talk to a parent and/or a school counselor to get the ball rolling. A diagnostic assessment can give you the clarity you need, and from there you can design the best academic plan that works with you, not against you.

Healthy High Achievers

Healthy high achievers are motivated by interest, curiosity, and sometimes passion. When they're passionate about something, they give it more time and attention because passion is their fuel. When they aren't passionate about something, they do their best to have a good attitude and make a strong effort but adjust their expectations accordingly.

Gemma, age 21: I've always loved math, and I can work hours on all my math subjects because time disappears and there's just me and what I'm working on. English is hell for me. I struggle with it but I'm okay not being good at everything. In high school I thought I had to be, but I think that's a myth that sets girls up to feel bad about themselves. My goal is to learn the need-to-know in English and get through it. Math is different because I want my grades to reflect my level of effort and commitment. I'm very capable of getting great scores in math, and it feels right when my grades reflect that.

Healthy high achievers work hard and generally love learning and doing well. Whether it's sports, academics, or any other pursuit, they balance work with other important considerations such as sleep, rest, and other forms of self-care. Healthy high achievers are much less vulnerable to anxiety, burnout, crashes, and meltdowns. They work with a better attitude and enjoy a better mental and emotional state than perfectionists do. They know they are more than what they achieve, and so they bounce back after disappointments more easily.

Here are more characteristics that describe HHAs:

- They often (but not always) feel passionate about learning.

- They give themselves permission to acknowledge that they're not good at every subject and don't like every subject—and that's okay.

- They learn how much work they need to do without overworking to the point of exhaustion.

- They don't make procrastination a thing, and since they're realistic about what they want to do and how well they can do it, they are less driven to use procrastination as an avoidance tactic.

- They embrace the idea that sometimes good enough is good enough.

- They give more to the subjects they love the most.

- They often feel interested and engaged with what they're working on.

- They know when to take breaks and use breaks to nap, rest, or practice other forms of self-care.

- They don't sacrifice sleep.

- They support other people in being their best. They don't feel demoralized when others perform better than they do.

An HHA may feel a sting of jealousy if a classmate performs better, but the sting fades and doesn't devolve into a self-critical narrative.

To become an HHA, you need to trade working *harder* for working *smarter*. To work smarter, you start by taking time to make a study plan that's realistic. A realistic study plan leaves room for breaks and bedtime.

Taking time to strategize how you will approach your workload sets you up for a reasonable, organized process. A good process often leads to a good outcome, while an insane process often leads to an emotional meltdown. When you create your work strategy, consider these suggestions:

Plan. Make a timeline of due dates for each class and assignment.

Keep track of your tasks. Make notes on a calendar (your phone calendar or an old school calendar—whichever works best for you). Write not only your assignment, quiz, and exam dates but also, in a different color, the time you will give to working on them.

Add fun to your calendar. Write in your get-to items along with your have-to's, so birthday parties and self-care don't get bumped off your schedule.

Leave wiggle room. Know it's okay to occasionally replace a get-to (for example, fun with friends) with a have-to (like studying for finals), but don't make a regular habit of that or you'll lose healthy balance.

Be realistic about grades. Set realistic expectations for the grade you expect to get. Just because your best friend gets straight As doesn't mean that you will, and it doesn't mean that you need to. Just because your sibling is an academic freak show of high achievement doesn't mean that you're "less than" if you aren't. Many girls have gifts and qualities that are not the focus of a high school curriculum.

PROCRASTINATION

While both perfectionists and frustrated achievers are vulnerable to procrastination, all achievement styles occasionally—if not regularly—fall prey to it.

Procrastinators know they procrastinate. It's not a blind spot. They *feel* the foolishness in scrolling social media, checking out new music, and typing "best brownie recipe" into the search bar when they have a mountain of homework to do.

If you're like a lot of girls who procrastinate, you know you do it, you feel bad about it, yet you continue on with it anyway.

The worst part about putting off what you should be doing (in order to do meaningless stuff) is that you are, in reality, setting yourself up for anxiety. It's like you're flirting with it, winking at it, inviting it over for a make-out session. No more! It's time to take your procrastination habit more seriously. It is not self-loving and it is not self-care.

The most helpful path to overcoming procrastination is to focus on action. Procrastinators tend to be ruled by their thoughts:

It's too hard, It's too much, I don't know how to do it, I don't know how to start, I don't want to, What if I don't feel smart at this?

And their feelings:

I don't feel like it, I'm scared, I don't feel confident, I don't feel clear, I'm going to feel bored/overwhelmed/stupid/ miserable/stressed.

E Is for Effort

None of those thoughts and feelings are fun but getting stuck in them only makes life harder. Avoiding your work is like avoiding anything that makes you anxious:

Avoidance feeds the problem and starves the solution.

As you've learned, the solution is simple (if not easy): go toward, go toward, go toward. Misery lies in avoidance. The solution is time and effort. As it turns out, going toward that which you want to avoid gets things done and makes you feel great, not just in the small picture (like procrastination) but in the big picture (your life!).

Make friends with effort and the healthy stress that comes with it because, as you know, not all stress is bad.

Good Stress

Working hard at challenging things makes you stronger and, in fact, *you can't get stronger without challenging yourself!* If you freak out over any sign of stress or difficulty, you're making the assumption that everything should be easy for you. If you focus only on what is easy for you, you'll never grow. You'll never have one of the awesome moments of thinking *Wow! I did that! I'm proud of myself! What else can I do that I didn't think I could?*

Accept that stress is inevitable and not necessarily a precursor to an anxious meltdown. Those meltdowns come with having unrealistic expectations, being too busy, and/or avoiding the work that needs to be done.

When it comes to work-related stress, face it, focus on what needs to be done, get help when you need it, and work. It will do wonders for your life and your sense of personal power.

When you feel yourself getting stuck, lazy, whiny, avoidant, and distractible, it's time to dig deep and focus on your actions. People who are fulfilled create lives for themselves with their actions. You can hope, dream, and want all day, every day, but it is your actions that create the life you live.

Noodle This: Next time you feel the pull of procrastination, what would it be like to hold yourself accountable? Procrastination is fakey self-care. It may feel good in the moment but only because you're indulging denial. Instead, shut down your screen or whatever else you're using for avoidance and do something kind for yourself. Make a snack or a cup of tea, take a walk, and then walk toward your work. Without wanting to, without indulging hesitation, keep directing yourself toward, toward,

toward your work. You will find, like all procrastinators do, that facing the work is easier on you than avoiding it.

QUICK TIPS FOR TEST ANXIETY

If you suffer from test anxiety, you're definitely not alone. You understand the material, do well on the homework, but consistently underperform in testing situations. Ughh! So annoying! These tips can help you overcome it:

Prepare. If you haven't given prep enough time and effort, expecting to feel cool as a cucumber is unrealistic. Make sure to prepare and you'll feel more confident.

Take a practice test. Put yourself in as close an approximation to the actual test situation as you can. Your brain reacts well to practice and rewards you by interacting with your nervous system in a beneficial way. Rereading and highlighting gets you only so far. Practice gets you further in performance.

Visualize yourself taking the test. Imagine yourself feeling clear and confident, maintaining focus, moving through the content, and completing the test with a feeling of satisfaction. Do this as often as you want but especially do it the night before the test and the morning of the test. Your brain will think this visualization is reality and set up neural pathways to create the experience for you, so get into detail and especially tap into feeling clear, calm, and confident in your visualization. Then, IRL, go in and smash that test!

Create a positive belief. Tell yourself you're excited to take the test. You don't need to hammer in that you're anxious by repeating that to yourself over and over again, and telling your friends, telling your parents. Talk confidently about yourself and to yourself and others. Say, *Here goes! I'm going to give it my best!*

Breathing techniques are another way to calm your nervous system for testing. Tip 10 will cover breathing and lots more anxiety slayers to top off all you've already learned. Time for your final tip!

Move Forward with Anxiety Slayers

The best success story is the one you create about yourself, for yourself!

—Lucie Hemmen

Yay! You've made it through nine tips that are changing your relationship with yourself and anxiety. As you now know, anxiety isn't solved by a quick fix. There isn't a single strategy or magical cure that makes it go away. The gift (yes, gift!) of having anxiety is that to shrink it, you absolutely must focus on making yourself more powerful. It is the power you build—through knowledge, self-care, and anxiety-slaying strategies—that puts you in charge of anxiety.

Keep practicing your new ways of being until they become part of who you are and the way you live life. Remember: *Your brain rewires through practicing new habits.* New and improved habits create a new and improved you.

Since all your tip work is designed to build health and power, you might already be noticing that you're just plain happier. As you know, happiness is a by-product of focusing on the right things in life. If you make happiness a goal, you'll monitor it too closely and feel frustrated. But if you focus on building and maintaining health, in all the ways you've been learning, happiness will frequently visit and hang out for a while. When fear (or any other emotion) chases it out the door, you can refocus on your self-care and your anxiety slayers to reset your sense of well-being.

Now you absolutely know that your relationship with yourself serves as *the source* of all the love and goodness you experience and share with others. While most people like the *idea* of having a good relationship with themselves, the tip work you're doing is creating that reality every day! Since small efforts are what it's all about, appreciate and celebrate all your efforts—even the smallest ones.

Feeling good is the result of small efforts practiced every day.

As you continue to live your tip work, life may not be perfect, but you'll find your positive state of flow allows you to handle challenges better. Life's stressors and triggers have less power to knock you down and steal your mood.

Knowing the importance of self-care will help you encourage others to practice it too. Teen girls often talk about "mom meltdowns" that occur when moms of teens do too much for others without taking enough time for themselves. If you see a parent, sibling, or friend walking the ragged edge of stress, share the message you're learning. We all need a little prompting and support to take better care of ourselves: *Mom, you do so much for everyone. I bet it feels endless and unrewarded. I appreciate you! And I think it's time to do something really nice for yourself.*

Who knows, maybe you'll both end up with a pedicure or a frozen yogurt!

Not only can you inspire people by example, you can remind them that self-care is restorative for everybody. Far from self-indulgent, it's a necessity in order to live a life of quality over chaos.

Now for the final fun. You've met many teens and college-age women who've shared their thoughts and lives with you. Now we'll revisit some of those women so you can hear their stories of personal success, as well as their favorite go-to anxiety-slaying techniques.

It's good to know as many anxiety slayers as possible because you'll find that some work better than others, and they can be used in creative combinations. Try as many as possible, create a few of your own, and compile a hearty inventory of favorites that become your go-to's.

TAKE A BREATHER

Okay, before you read on, take a deep breath and open your mind. This is a great anxiety slayer—one of the best—but it's an anxiety slayer that makes people (frequently) fight urges to smack the person suggesting it:

Are you %*#@ing kidding me right now?! I'm suffering, you demon! Telling me to inhale and exhale is like telling a drowning person to think happy thoughts. I might as well wait for a magical %*$#@ unicorn to fart rainbows on me. Get out of my face with your feeble suggestions. I may be dying!

It just doesn't tend to be a tip people get excited about. In the face of feeling really anxious, the suggestion to "just breathe" sounds too simple to be powerful—like spitting on a fire. But here's the thing: when you understand *why* breathing exercises work, you *may* be more open to embracing this slayer.

Nerd Alert: Breathing exercises work on anxiety by disrupting your body's fight-flight-freeze response. Remember that when your brain interprets a threat, your body ramps up to fight full-on or to run for your life.

173

Blood flow changes, heart rate changes, muscle tone changes, *respiration changes*.

You want to reset respiration because when you do, the rest of your system follows that cue. A solid, well-practiced breathing exercise quickly and effectively derails the A train of anxiety.

When you engage in an exercise such as square breathing or alternate nostril breathing, you not only give your mind a distraction from anxious thoughts, you are *slowing your heart rate and soothing your entire nervous system.*

And the improvement you get is immediate! Because breathing exercises are a physiological fix for your body's system-wide freak-out, they are extremely effective with no downside, other than the resistance people feel to *believing in them!*

Do an internet search for "square breathing," "alternate nostril breathing," or even "best breathing exercises for anxiety." There's a wealth of info out there, and you'll even find some video tutorials to help get you breathing like the chillest person on earth.

Practice those suckers every day. Just as a firefighter learns to use a firehose *before* an actual fire, so must you master your "breathers" *before* your moment of need. Then, when you feel triggered by anxiety, you can engage one of your favorites as easily and naturally as a firefighter engages their hose. With similar results!

Remember Miranda from Tip 1? She slayed her air travel anxiety like an absolute boss. She flew to Australia (a very long flight) and arrived tired, but with a feeling she could do anything. It was her biggest fear and she slayed it from dragon to gecko status.

Miranda's update: Okay, so I started off by googling images of the plane, the flight route, etc. Then I talked to an actual pilot who answered a bunch of questions on safety of air travel. Then I practiced square breathing everyday ... many times. I practiced first thing in the morning, in the shower, during volleyball practice and games, before tests, during tests, when I watched my shows ... I'm a professional square breather. I'm gonna work that into my college apps. (Laughing) I became so good at my square breathing that it was natural to do it before the flight, on the flight, during turbulence. I never got too wound up. Breathing is something you always have no matter what. and it works. It gives me confidence knowing that I have something that easy and available I can use anytime.

Anchor your breathing practice to things you do each day. Every morning when you wake up, practice a breathing exercise. Every night before you go to sleep, practice. Then choose at least one additional time: maybe in the shower or while walking or driving. In class is also a great time because your breathing exercises are between you and you.

Unless you're doing alternate nostril breathing (which is especially great during a panic attack), no one will notice you're doing anything different than just sitting there. Embrace, engage, and enjoy the power of taking a very special breather.

Bonus breather: You know those nights when you're trying to go to sleep but your mind is like a monkey swinging from branch to branch? Try this visualization/breathing exercise:

Think of a pleasant memory from your life. It can be old or recent. Now try to remember each and every detail you can about the memory. Enjoy leaning into the details and notice the feelings in your body. As you notice various feelings, pause and focus on your

breathing. Count six seconds on your inhale and eight seconds on
your exhale as you focus on the pleasant feeling or feelings. Then go
on to more of the memory or choose another memory.

As you explore this exercise, know that you can't do it wrong. Any way you tweak it is fine. You may pause lots of mindful inhales and exhales, or skip that part entirely and focus exclusively on each morsel of the memory that you can recall and enjoy. If other feelings come up, note them and go back to the memory or go on to another.

Think of your mind as a monkey you can train. If it's all over the tree causing trouble, you can learn to direct it where you'd like it to go. Additionally, this exercise reminds you that feelings very often follow thoughts. It's good to practice feeling good! Just imagine every cell of your body retuning its energy to sync with the good feelings you're inviting in.

TRICK ANXIETY WITH YOUR BODY

Social scientists have long examined the impact human body language has on others. More recently, they've begun to examine the effects our own body language has on us. How crazy is that? Your body language not only affects the way other people experience you, it affects the way you experience yourself!

We convey a lot with our bodies, without knowing it. When you feel unsure and intimidated, your body will naturally take on those emotions and reveal them. Conversely, when you walk with awareness and confidence, you not only cue others that you're strong and confident—you cue yourself.

Nerd Alert: Search Amy Cuddy's TED Talk "Your Body Language May Shape Who You Are." It's a really interesting and touching talk, plus you'll get the need-to-know on how you can use body language to shape how you feel.

Remember Madi from Tip 3, who was bullied in middle school and is now a sophomore in high school? Here's her success story.

I think a lot of things helped me get through what I call my dark years. Learning how to stop being so hard on myself with my self-talk was big. I stopped hating on myself and created a better way of thinking about myself and talking to myself internally. I'd catch myself thinking all the worst-case scenarios about what other people were thinking of me, and I had to work consistently on training away from those thoughts and toward better thoughts.

My older sister always told me to "fake it 'til you make it" but I never really knew what she meant until one day, we had a long talk and she really told me. She said when she feels really intimidated by a situation, she just pretends she's super confident and barges into things. She got a job that way. She walked into this restaurant that was opening and said she wanted to work there, that she didn't have any experience but was a fast learner. She said she acted very bubbly and outgoing and that made her feel bubbly and outgoing. They hired her. She said when she walked in that day, she literally told her feet to keep walking toward the manager. I guess that tricks you into thinking you're okay or something like that.

So I started doing the same thing. I started off talking to the kids in class without thinking about it. I'd just pretend that I was confident because my sister convinced me that no one actually knows what you're feeling inside. Then I built on that over time, just making friendly gestures to people around me—even randoms at school that I didn't know, like compliments on their presentations or whatever. Nothing deep, just contact until I wasn't anxious about it anymore. Instead of pulling my eyes away from people, I started keeping eye contact. It's like I literally built myself into more of a confident person, and it doesn't make me feel fake at all. It makes me feel more myself actually.

Embrace exploring a braver part of you that you may not know exists with this fake-it practice: Pick a place in your life where you want to experiment showing a level of confidence you may not actually feel. It can be a social situation, a performance situation, and even a phobia.

Then go somewhere that you have privacy and practice strong and confident body movements. Allow them to be very dramatic and over the top—just so that you break out of the box you've felt stuck in. Go ahead and laugh as you explore a new relationship with that which you've feared.

This is what Madi did:

Oh, I used all the confidence hacks. I was ridiculous and would make myself laugh but it worked and still works for me. I practiced walking with confidence and talking with confidence. I share a room with my little sister, so I'd go into the garage when no one was around and practice victory arms and taking up space. I actually still do victory arms but before tests and usually in bathroom stalls. (Laughing) I say, "Yes! I've got this!" When I really work with my body language, the rest of me feels better. I do the leaning–in thing too where you shift your weight forward when you're actually feeling a little nervous. Like at a meeting with my college counselor when I was nervous, I found myself leaning back and folding my arms, and then I quickly changed my posture to be straighter and leaned forward a little. Then I had an easier time feeling confident and comfortable.

These strategies work because their focus is on behavior, not feelings or thoughts. When you're trying to be brave and break out of fear, focus on your behavior and tell your body what to do. While important in many situations, thoughts and feelings can hold you back when you're feeling scared or intimidated.

If you know you're safe and that what you're trying to achieve is good for you, *focus on behavior. Action, action, action.*

Try these hacks:

Lean in. Notice the way you sit in your chair. When you want to feel more comfortable and confident, unfold your arms and legs, sit up straight, and lean forward in an interested and engaged manner. See how it feels!

Use victory arms. Amy Cuddy's TED Talk will inspire you to explore victory arms for yourself. Explore being powerful and see how it affects your mood and confidence.

Soften, don't contract. When you feel nervous or anxious, it's natural to contract the muscles in your body. Become aware of that tensing, and practice softening those contracted muscles. One way to become aware is to notice what happens when you sit down somewhere. Are you giving the weight of your body to the chair, or are your muscles still contracted? You may be surprised at how much unnecessary clenching your muscles do. Softening your contraction habit often softens anxiety and enhances feelings of safety and wellbeing. Easy and worth investigating!

Take up space. While boys and men tend to take up space with their bodies, girls and women often do the opposite—without even realizing it. Start noticing how you walk through the world and how you sit. When you're in environments that intimidate you, notice how your body moves and takes up space (or doesn't). Explore making subtle changes in a bolder, more space-consuming direction, and see how these adjustments make you feel.

Do the opposite. This is a suggestion you need to try in order to truly understand. Remember Chloe from Tip 5, who shared that 75 percent of her wanted to drive but the 25 percent of her that felt scared seemed more powerful and intense? Well, she used this strategy to unstick herself from that 25 percent. One day when her mom suggested (for the hundredth time) that they should practice, she felt her no but said "Yes, how about now?" Her dad looked at her, surprised, and off they went. It was so empowering and liberating for Chloe that she used this hack for many things she didn't want to but knew she had to:

Now I just know that whenever I feel like I don't want to do something—like homework or cleaning my room—I just don't take that seriously and I get moving fast, like I'm escaping a giant suction that wants to resist. It's easier to do than to resist.

Get to know these hacks by picturing situations in which you'd use each one. Your body feels so much happier when it's promoting your growth and happiness than when it's resisting and withdrawing.

LOOK FOR YOUR SECOND REACTION

You know that moment when someone asks something of you and you feel that on-the-spot rush of anxiety? Maybe it's a teacher calling on you in class or someone asking you a question that takes you by surprise. Maybe it's being asked to do something social. Whatever the circumstance, you feel a spike of anxiety because you feel resistance and possibly fear in the face of responding.

This is sometimes called the "spotlight effect" because when it strikes, you feel a spotlight on you that amplifies everything. Luckily, no one else sees the spotlight you feel. It's an internal experience that you can shift yourself out of as soon as you know how.

Emotions are energy *in* motion. They have movement, and often the first feelings on the scene are the wildest and noisiest. When you notice them, get good at reminding yourself: *Feelings have movement. This is my first feeling, but if I pause and calm myself, other thoughts, feelings, and perspectives will reveal themselves to me.*

Then have a quick talk with your body, especially your muscles, which are probably clenching and tense: *Soften body, soften muscles. No danger here. This can be handled. I've got this.*

When you take time to settle and observe the movement of emotions, you'll be in better shape to think well about ways to move forward. Self-talk like the example above helps noisy emotions settle so that calmer ones can take charge.

If a response still doesn't come, articulate a space filler to create more space for yourself. For example:

- *Sorry, what was your question?*

- *Hmmm, I'm not sure right now.*

- *I need a minute to think about it.*

- *I need to check my schedule.*

Since everybody gets distracted or flustered sometimes, you're unlikely to be judged for any of those space fillers. Remember, you're here to grow and learn and love. You're not here to be perfect.

Sometimes a space filler gives you time to meet, greet, and welcome your *second reaction*, a reaction that is less constricted by fear. It's not a flinch response, it's a true response.

Zaya, age 22: The best thing I ever learned to help with those anxious spikes is to wait for my second reaction. Or what I actually do is look for my second reaction. My first reaction was a freeze response because I was so afraid of being awkward that I made a lot of things awkward. When I learned the "emotions have movement" thing, I learned to feel the terrified spike, then immediately look for my second

reaction. It always came! So in a class, for example, I'd feel frozen, remind myself there was another reaction, find it, and move forward. That was especially helpful for being called on in class or having to give presentations. I noticed that the eternity between my first and second reaction became shorter and shorter. It's like, when you trust that there's more than panic available for you, your panic lasts two seconds and then a helpful response comes faster.
Or guys—when a cute guy said something to me, I'd freeze for a second, look for my second reaction, and then move forward like a reasonable person. It's totally an inside, more subtle thing to explore, but it's worth exploring. Now that I'm a senior in college, I find when people ask me to do things my first response is most often "I don't want to" but instead of getting caught up, I tell people I need to check my schedule and in the time that takes, my actual response comes to me. Sometimes it's yes and sometimes it's no—but it's never that automatic yes or no that's driven by anxiety.
Oh yeah, for girls learning this, it's key to relax your muscles the instant you feel that anxiety. You will actually train anxiety to only last a second because when you unscrunch your shoulders or whatever is tensing, you'll pivot yourself right out of the anxiety spike.

Nerd Alert: Like Zaya says, emotions have movement. Just because fear arrives first doesn't mean it's the only visitor. Other feelings are often right behind it. Give your spike of anxiety a quick nod, relax what is tensing in your body—and look for what's next. In class, maybe it's the correct answer or a simple "I'm not sure of the answer."

When taken by surprise in some other scenario, often a reasonable answer is directly behind the spike of fear, so work on not taking the spike too seriously and the answer will come more quickly.

USE YOUR IMAGINATION

One of anxiety's favorite tricks is to hijack your imagination and use it against you. You want to talk to someone you're attracted to, but your imagination creates a scenario of making a fool of yourself—which affects your behavior—and you back off.

Or you'd like to run for student council and think you'd do a great job, but your imagination steals your optimistic vibes and replaces them with a blown-up and catastrophized failure scenario that has you convinced it's best not to even try.

Since you have a great imagination, you might as well use it for your benefit by exploring visualization.

Remember Lexi from Tip 1, who shared that anxiety makes her head feel like "a beehive… weirdly buzzy"? She used her imagination to visualize a circle around her anxiety. Since her favorite color is pink and she likes sparkles, she visualized a pink, sparkly circle. Whenever she felt the beehive effect, Lexi made a practice out of surrounding the buzzy feelings with the pink circle and then, with every exhale, shrinking the circle (and the buzzy feelings) one exhale at a time.

Here's what she says:

This is my best anxiety slayer because the buzzy head thing can put me into a really bad mood, and I was getting it a lot in math, to the point I couldn't focus on the teacher. So I have my pink circle thing (laughing) and I practice shrinking it with my out–breath until the buzzy feeling is really small and then it pops like a bubble. No one knows I'm doing it, and since I do it slowly, I can still focus in class. I end up really calm and my mind feels clear. Oh yeah, on the in–breath, I just focus on relaxing.

Lexi uses her imagination to shrink the physical manifestation of anxiety in her body. If you feel anxiety in your stomach or chest or even all over, personalize Lexi's anxiety slayer to suit you and give it a try. It's great at bedtime because it gives the monkeys something to do that's calming—so they don't get into trouble!

You can also use your imagination to practice doing something that intimidates you. If you've got a presentation to do in class, you can visualize walking to the front of the room feeling completely prepared and even excited to share your presentation. You can imagine your body feeling calm and your eye contact with the class feeling strong and natural. You can imagine your voice sounding clear and steady. The more detail, the better.

If you want to go to a social event and feel confident and friendly, you can use visualization to prime yourself to be your best social self. By closing your eyes and imagining just how you'd feel, sound, look, speak, move in your body, you're working on creating exactly what you want.

Nerd Alert: Visualization works because neurons in your brain interpret imagery as equivalent to a real-life experience. Whether you visualize yourself shrinking your physical symptoms of anxiety or you visualize yourself slaying your presentation, your brain generates impulses that tell your neurons to perform the actions involved. New neural pathways (clusters of cells that work together to create learned behaviors) then prime you to act in accordance with your visualization.

Also, when you're visualizing yourself doing something, you do that thing without mistakes. That's why elite athletes use it to maximize their performance. When a pole vaulter imagines herself executing her moves, she imagines herself doing every piece of the vault perfectly and her brain records that information.

When it's time for her event, her brain and body are aligned for success. Golfers use this strategy a lot, as do athletes and performers of all kinds. You can use visualization to help yourself execute brave acts, or you can use it to get power over anxiety. The possibilities are as limitless as your fabulous imagination.

Write On

Congratulations for moving through these ten tips that were created especially for you. It's a perfect time to grab your journal and list anxiety slayers you want to try and practice. Keep working on your new habits, and make sure to celebrate the improvements you notice over time. Your very last tip is to embrace the following mantra and repeat it to yourself often, because it's true!

I am getting better and better, stronger and stronger. Every day, I practice kindness to myself and kindness to others.

References

Alter, A. 2017. "Why Our Screens Make Us Less Happy." TED video.
    Accessed April 2017. https://www.ted.com/talks/adam_alter_why
    _our screens_make_us_less_happy.

Betancourt, J. 2018. California: Health Coach Institute. https://www.facebook
    .com/jessica.betancourt.33671.

Bolte, T. J. 2008. *My Stroke of Insight*. New Jersey: Penguin Group.

Brown, B. 2018. "Brené Brown on Joy and Gratitude." Global Leadership
    Network. https://globalleadership.org/articles/leading-yourself/brene
    -brown-on-joy-and-gratitude.

Crawford, K. 2019. "Tuning Out: What Happens when You Drop Facebook."
    Stanford, CA: Stanford Institute for Economic Policy Research (SIEPR).
    https://siepr.stanford.edu/news/drop-facebook.

Cuddy, A. 2012. "Your Body Language May Shape Who You Are."
    TED video. Accessed November 2019. https://www.youtube.com/watch
    ?v=Ks-_Mh1QhMc.

Environmental Protection Agency. "Indoor Air Quality: What are the
    trends in indoor air quality and their effects on human health?"
    Accessed January 5, 2020. https://www.epa.gov/report-environment
    /indoor-air-quality.

Gaunce, C. 2020. Recovery and Support. "Websites with Information on
    Eating Disorders." http://www.christinalynnrd.com/resources/information
    -on-eating-disorders.

Gladwell, M. 2013. *David and Goliath*. New York: Little Brown and Company.

Harris, T. 2014. "How Better Tech Could Protect Us from Distraction."
    TED video. Accessed December, 2019. https://www.ted.com/talks
    /tristan_harris_how_better_tech_could_protect_us_from_distraction.

Kabat-Zinn, J. 2005. *Wherever You Go, There You Are.* New York: Hachette Books.

Schwartz, R. C. 2018. *Greater Than the Sum of Our Parts.* Louisville, CO: Sounds True Inc.

Twenge, J. 2018. "Teens Today Spend More Time on Digital Media, Less Time Reading." American Psychological Association. https://www.apa.org/news/press/releases/2018/08/teenagers-read-book.

Lucie Hemmen, PhD, is a licensed clinical psychologist in private practice who specializes in working with teens and their parents while raising two teen girls of her own, Marley and Daisy. She is author of *Parenting a Teen Girl* and *The Teen Girl's Survival Guide*.

More Instant Help Books for Teens

An Imprint of New Harbinger Publications

**THE TEEN GIRL'S
SURVIVAL GUIDE**

Ten Tips for Making Friends,
Avoiding Drama & Coping
with Social Stress

978-1626253063 / US $17.95

**PUT YOUR
WORRIES HERE**

A Creative Journal for
Teens with Anxiety

978-1684032143 / US $17.95

**GOODNIGHT MIND
FOR TEENS**

Skills to Help You Quiet
Noisy Thoughts & Get
the Sleep You Need

978-1684034383 / US $16.95

EXPRESS YOURSELF

A Teen Girl's Guide to Speaking
Up & Being Who You Are

978-1626251489 / US $17.95

**THE SELF-LOVE
REVOLUTION**

Radical Body Positivity
for Girls of Color

978-1684034116 / US $16.95

**THE ANXIETY
WORKBOOK FOR TEENS**

Activities to Help You Deal
with Anxiety & Worry

978-1572246034 / US $17.95

 newharbingerpublications

1-800-748-6273 / newharbinger.com

(VISA, MC, AMEX / prices subject to change without notice)

Follow Us 🄾 f 🄳 ▶ 🄿 in

Don't miss out on new books in the subjects that interest you.
Sign up for our **Book Alerts** at **newharbinger.com/bookalerts**